What is Discourse Analysis?

D1352308

### 'What is?' Research Methods series

Edited by Graham Crow, University of Southampton
ISSN: 2048–6812

The 'What is?' series provides authoritative introductions to a range of research methods which are at the forefront of developments in the social sciences. Each volume sets out the key elements of the particular method and features examples of its application, drawing on a consistent structure across the whole series. Written in an accessible style by leading experts in the field, this series is an innovative pedagogical and research resource.

**What is Online Research?**
*Tristram Hooley, Jane Wellens and John Marriott*

**What is Social Network Analysis?**
*John Scott*

**What is Qualitative Research?**
*Martyn Hammersley*

**What are Qualitative Research Ethics?**
*Rose Wiles*

**What are Community Studies?**
*Graham Crow*

**Forthcoming books:**

**What is Qualitative Interviewing?**
*Rosalind Edwards and Janet Holland*

**What is Narrative Research?**
*Molly Andrews, Mark Davis, Cigdem Esin, Lar-Christer Hyden, Margareta Hyden, Corinne Squire and Barbara Harrison*

**What is Inclusive Research?**
*Melanie Nind*

# What is discourse analysis?

Stephanie Taylor

B L O O M S B U R Y

LONDON • NEW DELHI • NEW YORK • SYDNEY

**Bloomsbury Academic**

An imprint of Bloomsbury Publishing Plc

| 50 Bedford Square | 175 Fifth Avenue |
|---|---|
| London | New York |
| WC1B 3DP | NY 10010 |
| UK | USA |

**www.bloomsbury.com**

First published 2013

No responsibility for loss caused to any individual or organization acting on or refraining
from action as a result of the material in this publication can be accepted by Bloomsbury
Academic or the author.

**British Library Cataloguing-in-Publication Data**
A catalogue record for this book is available from the British Library.

ISBN: HB: 978-1-7809-3849-3

PB: 978-1-8496-6903-0

ePub: 978-1-8496-6906-1

ePDF: 978-1-8496-6905-4

**Library of Congress Cataloging-in-Publication Data**
A catalog record for this book is available from the Library of Congress.

Typeset by Newgen Imaging Systems Pvt, Ltd, Chennai, India

# Contents

# Series foreword

The idea behind this series is a simple one: to provide concise and accessible overviews of a range of frequently used research methods and of current issues in research methodology. Books in the series have been written by experts in their fields, following a brief, to write about their subject for a broad audience who are assumed to be interested but not necessarily to have any prior knowledge. The series is a natural development of presentations made in the 'What is?' strand at Economic and Social Research Council (ESRC) Research Methods Festivals which have proved popular both at the Festivals themselves and subsequently as a resource on the website of the ESRC National Centre for Research Methods. Methodological innovation is the order of the day, and the 'What is?' format allows researchers who are new to a field to gain an insight into its key features, while also providing a useful update on recent developments for people who have had some prior acquaintance with it. All readers should find it helpful to be taken through the discussion of key terms, the history of how the method or methodological issue has developed and the assessment of the strengths and possible weaknesses of the approach through analysis of illustrative examples.

Discourse analysis was an obvious choice for inclusion in the series because it is a vital method for understanding a key aspect of social life, namely what people say and how they say it. Making sense of patterns of communication is by no means as straightforward as might be imagined, for even apparently mundane everyday exchanges have hidden dimensions to them that discourse analysis has the capacity to reveal. It can be controversial to explore the ways in which things that are routinely treated as 'just talk' are much more important and interesting than that, because discourse analysis has the potential to highlight issues of power and the creation and contestation of meaning, but the association of controversy with a method may be taken as an indication of its capacity to go beyond comfortable but superficial understandings. Discourse analysis certainly encourages us to think differently, and in this book Stephanie Taylor's careful exposition of the method reveals the insights that can be gained by doing so.

The books cannot provide information about their subject matter down to a fine level of detail, but they will equip readers with a powerful sense of reasons why it deserves to be taken seriously and, it is hoped, with the enthusiasm to put that knowledge into practice.

*Graham Crow*
*Series editor*

# Acknowledgements

I would like to thank the many colleagues and students who have contributed to my own understanding and use of qualitative research methods, including discourse analysis, in discussions at the Open University and elsewhere, especially Margaret Wetherell, Martyn Hammersley, Jean McAvoy, Karen Littleton and the members of the Discourse Group and Qualitative Work in Progress Group. I would also like to thank Meg Barker, Martyn Hammersley (again) and Jovan Byford for their invaluable feedback on the manuscript in progress. This book is dedicated to the memory of Jill Reynolds who was a friend, colleague and co-author and is sadly missed by the Qualitative Work in Progress Group here at the Open University.

# 1 Introduction

This book has been written as an introduction, to explain and demonstrate some of the possibilities which discourse analysis offers for contemporary social research. It is for novices as well as experienced researchers in the social sciences and related disciplines who want to read about other people's discourse analytic research and perhaps conduct their own similar projects. The two major themes of the book are as follows: discourse analysis does not refer to a single approach or method, and its varied forms cannot be distinguished without an understanding of their premises. The aim is therefore to help readers understand the connections between the theoretical assumptions which a discourse researcher makes about the social world, the research topic or problem being investigated, the data chosen for analysis and the aspects of the data which are studied. Any research project represents a unique combination of these features, and indeed part of the attraction of discourse analysis is the wide range of possibilities which it encompasses.

Chapter 1 develops an initial definition of discourse analysis and then outlines the content of the subsequent chapters, with some suggestions for using the book effectively as a practical guide, and building on its content.

## What is discourse analysis?

This question is difficult to answer succinctly because the term 'discourse analysis' refers to a range of approaches in several disciplines and theoretical traditions. Discourse analysts in sociolinguistics, sociology and social psychology, to mention just a few possibilities, are likely to differ in the sources they refer to, and also, to some extent, in the problems and research questions which they set out to investigate. This variety is potentially confusing, but also positive in that it expands the possibilities for new researchers and projects. This book provides an overview of discourse analytic research as a rich and interdisciplinary field which continues to change and develop in new directions. Later chapters will discuss some of the theoretical background and examples of research studies. This section begins a discussion on the meaning of the term discourse analysis.

One starting point is that discourse analysis usually refers to a research approach in which language material, such as talk or written texts, and sometimes other material altogether, is examined as evidence of phenomena *beyond the individual person*. To understand this, imagine looking at some old letters, written several decades or even centuries ago. Each letter will of course be interesting for what it conveys about the writer's situation, opinions and feelings. However, it can also provide more general evidence of society at that earlier time. For instance, passing references may suggest what is taken for granted, including the priorities and values shared by members of society. Some of the words used may even be offensive to a contemporary reader, for instance, because they are linked to assumptions about class or gender or race which have since been questioned. In addition, some of the writing may seem 'old-fashioned' in its style and level of formality because there have been changes in the directness with which people express opinions or state disagreements. If letters between both parties to the correspondence have survived, they will provide further insights into how people communicated at that time, including the conventions which operate in particular relationships, business or personal. In short, each letter, however private its original purpose, is potentially of interest as evidence of social phenomena, in a way that the writer could not have anticipated. This is the level of interpretation employed by a discourse analyst.

To explain the variety of discourse analytic research, it is useful to distinguish two lines of academic work. They do not encompass all the variations in discourse analysis and in practice, they tend to converge particularly around the study of difference and inequality and the workings of power in society, as some of the studies discussed later in the book will indicate. Nonetheless, the distinction is helpful as a starting point.

The focus of the first line of academic work is the nature of language. Traditionally, linguistics, or 'linguistics proper', can be defined narrowly as 'the study of "grammar" in a broad sense: the sound systems of language ("phonology"), the grammatical structure of words ("morphology") and of sentences ("syntax") and more formal aspects of meaning ("semantics")' (Fairclough, 2001a, p. 5). However, sociolinguists and many other academics consider language as inseparable from its social contexts. Among many other aspects of language use, they study differences in how people speak (and write) which are linked to class and other social categories, or to a particular activity, situation, role and purpose. Summarized somewhat crudely, this line of writing and research can therefore be said to have extended from the concerns of 'linguistics proper' to explore features of language linked, again, to social phenomena. Discourse analytic research in this line includes investigations of the details of how language varies across contexts and can mark social difference, and how children acquire competence in language use and, again, how that competence is linked to identity and social difference.

The second academic line can be said to have originated in the study of society and people as social beings, especially in sociology and social psychology, and then developed to incorporate a focus on language. In other words, the move has been in the opposite direction, from social phenomena to language. For example, discourse researchers have analysed public and private language use as a way of accessing the collective, though not necessarily coherent, 'world view' of a society. Some aspects would be the ways in which people and their activities are categorized, valued and located in relationships of dominance and subservience. Language use may also be analysed as one activity or practice (some would say, the most important practice) which people engage in as part of their ongoing social lives and relationships. Through the analysis of language and language use, the researcher therefore builds up a picture of society and how it functions.

The variety in discourse analytic research is also partly given by the kinds of data used by researchers. Discourse analysts can study other forms of representation from language, such as pictures and film, or consider language use alongside other practices, but most work with some kind of language data (the focus of this book). Some researchers investigate historical material, like the old letters already mentioned, but most take as their data contemporary material related to language and communication. As already noted, this is analysed following the principle that language provides evidence of social phenomena. For example talk, perhaps from focus groups or people participating in interviews, will be of interest not (just) as straightforward reporting, like witness statements. (Many analysts will also avoid interpreting it as a direct report of the speaker's inner thought processes and feelings.) Instead, the analysis may focus on how the interaction of speakers is shaped and constrained by its social contexts, from the immediate conversational interaction to the larger situation of the place, time, state of the nation and so on. The analysis may explore the styles of speaking, and the 'to and fro' of the talk. It may consider the details of how the talk is constructed, including grammatically, and the implications of the choice of one possible word or structure over an alternative. It may consider the functions of the talk, or examine the assumptions which apparently underlie what is said. Words, expressions and arguments may be analysed as social and cultural resources associated with certain social groups and contexts, recycled and modified by individual language users in particular instances of communication. The analysis may explore more dramatic aspects of the talk, for instance, when someone speaks 'as' a certain character or role (a concerned parent, an authoritative expert) or appears to repeat a well-rehearsed anecdote, or address an audience beyond the immediate situation. Some of these foci are associated with particular named approaches to discourse analysis, but in many or even the majority of studies, the features to be studied will be decided according to the priorities of the research, drawing on the wide range of possibilities given by previous published work.

The remainder of this book looks more closely at some of these possibilities. To assist the exploration, it will be useful to give an initial answer to the question 'What is discourse analysis?' as follows: *Discourse analysis is the close study of language and language use as evidence of aspects of society and social life.* Later chapters of the book return to this definition and extend it.

## The chapters

Chapter 2, 'Theories and common concerns', presents an overview of the main theoretical traditions relevant to discourse analysis in the social sciences. Although the focus is on key ideas, not individual theorists, the chapter does introduce some of the 'names' readers may encounter in their reading of other sources. It is intended as a starting point for further reading which researchers can build on as they follow their own interests and develop new projects.

Chapter 3, 'Four examples of discourse analysis', discusses four recent articles published in academic journals, each of which presents findings from a discourse analytic study. The examples have been chosen to demonstrate the variety of discourse analytic approaches and also of the kinds of research problems they have been used to address. Together, the four articles refer to a range of subject fields, project designs and types of data. The first article, by Kirsten Bell, is based on a study conducted with people attending cancer support groups; the second, by Jovan Byford, on an investigation of political rhetoric; the third, by Elizabeth Stokoe, on a close analysis of talk from neighbours engaged in disputes; and the fourth, by Ruth Wodak, Winston Kwon and Ian Clarke, on a study of meetings in a business organization. The four articles variously discuss racism and prejudice, health, risk and personal responsibility, morality and gender, and leadership and consensus. The chapter provides an overview of each research project, its theoretical grounding, the empirical work and the data which were analysed, and the discourse analytic or discursive approach which the researcher has adopted.

Chapter 4, 'The usefulness of discourse analysis for social science researchers', begins with a general discussion of the reasons for using this form of research and for analysing language data. The chapter also discusses two 'half-reasons' which are based on a partial misunderstanding of the premises of a discourse analytic approach. The chapter then describes some of the different kinds of data which can be analysed discursively and considers practical aspects of obtaining discourse data. The chapter includes sections on the collection of new data, the selection of already existing or 'found' material as data and the production of transcripts.

Chapter 5 considers some of the problems or challenges faced by the discourse analyst. These include deciding on the right discourse analytic approach, and beginning to analyse data and develop an interpretation and argument. The discussions of interpretation and analysis continue the practical guidance provided in Chapter 4.

Every research approach has its critics and Chapter 6 addresses some common criticisms of discourse analysis. For example, the chapter answers the challenges sometimes made that discourse analysis is out of date as an approach or is 'just' about words, or that it does not take enough account of people or has limited practical applications. The chapter also discusses some more specific criticisms, such as that discourse analysts should not collect data through interviews.

Chapter 7 summarizes the key points covered in previous chapters and presents a list of suggestions and references for readers who would like to build on the practical introduction to discourse analysis which is presented in this book. The book also includes a glossary of key terms.

## Using this book

Like other text books, 'What is discourse analysis?' has been written as a guide and reference tool. Readers are likely to turn to chapters and sections which seem pertinent to their immediate concerns and practical problems. However, the book has also been written to be read from start to finish. The concepts and terms which are introduced in Chapter 2 are referred to in the very detailed discussions of empirical studies presented in Chapter 3. The discussions in Chapters 4 and 5 refer back to those studies, and to previous chapters, and the arguments presented in Chapter 6 presume some awareness of theories and concepts introduced earlier in the book. Readers are therefore recommended to work through the chapters in order, at least initially. It will also be useful to refer to the glossary of key terms at the end of the book.

## Summary

Chapter 1 has introduced the topic of the book, offered an initial answer to the question 'What is discourse analysis?' and outlined the contents of the remaining chapters.

# 2 Theories and common concerns

## Introduction

Chapter 1 proposed a definition of discourse analysis as 'the close study of language and language use as evidence of aspects of society and social life'. This chapter explores the theoretical underpinnings of discourse analysis and some of the main concerns of researchers, including the different terms they use. The first three sections will discuss theories which establish a connection between language and social phenomena and therefore inform discourse researchers' arguments for the status of language data as evidence. The fourth section discusses some relevant terminology, including different definitions of the key term 'discourse'. The fifth and sixth sections introduce some of the most important concerns which underlie discourse analytic research in different traditions, and the seventh section outlines the links between discourse analysis and social psychology.

To introduce the first two sections, it may be useful to return to the example of letters, introduced in Chapter 1. The discussion there of course assumed that readers understand what is meant by 'a letter', even though the use of letters is increasingly superseded by electronic communications. A formal dictionary definition, from the *Shorter Oxford Dictionary* (1965), is that a letter is 'a missive in writing, an epistle', a definition which might prompt further consultation of dictionaries. A simpler definition is that a letter is a communication on paper which is conventionally sent through a postal system. This probably explains the 'meaning' of a letter sufficiently for someone to understand what the word refers to, for instance, in order to translate it from one language to another. However, it does not encompass the kinds of meanings which might be of interest to a social researcher. Consider, for example, the difference between using a letter or an email. A letter would probably seem more appropriate to an invitation for a special occasion. Similarly, in a personal relationship, especially one in its early stages, a love letter would probably carry greater significance than a declaration of love in an email. More negatively, in a correspondence about a dispute, perhaps in a workplace or between neighbours, sending a letter might raise the issue to a new level of seriousness. In short, a letter can carry meanings of formality and occasion (the invitation), commitment and lastingness (the love letter), seriousness and legality (the dispute). These meanings are cultural, made familiar through the many experiences of being part of a society, including seeing the post delivered, receiving letters and sending them, and reading or viewing stories in which letters mark key dramatic points. Additional meanings will attach to details like the quality of the paper, whether the letter is printed or handwritten and whether it is addressed to a named person or merely 'The Occupier'. And there are many other associations, of emotion and of images, such as a bundle of letters tied with red ribbon, a card decorated with balloons and so on.

These meanings and associations are not fixed. They have accumulated over time and may now be fading because of the increasing use of electronic communication. In addition, the meanings of particular letters will depend on their context, including the context of a time (today, 20 years ago or a few years into the future), the purpose of the letter, and the relationship between the sender and recipient(s). The relevant point for this discussion is that a letter is not *just* a letter but potential data for a social researcher. It may provide evidence relevant to the exploration of society and social phenomena such as celebrations, or changes in intimate relationships, or the settlement of disputes, or institutionalized communication or the legal profession: the exact focus will be given by the topic which the researcher has chosen to investigate.

This example need not be elaborated any further but it introduces the three approaches to meaning which will be discussed in the following sections, in relation to language. The first is the exploration of social meanings as systems or aggregates, accrued over time. The second is the study of meaningful practices, such as inviting, declaring, threatening and also writing, signing, witnessing, consulting a lawyer, entering a contract and many more. The third concerns the use of language for the communication of meanings. All three sections adopt a broad approach and at some points juxtapose theorists who are usually associated with separate traditions of academic work. As indicated in Chapter 1, the aim is to introduce the field and enable readers to begin pursuing lines of interest to be followed up in further reading.

## Theorizing language as systems or aggregates of meanings

The example of the letters introduced the notion that there are aggregates or groups of meanings which 'hang together' by association rather than logical links. The theorization of such systems of meaning is strongly informed by the work of the French philosopher and social theorist Michel Foucault (1926–84). His work is perhaps less academically fashionable than it was two or three decades ago, but its influence persists, including in work which may not acknowledge it directly. Foucault's writings are too wide-ranging and complex to be summarized easily. His own research was primarily historical in the sense that he attempted to unravel the foundations of contemporary knowledge by tracking connections between ideas back through a variety of documentary sources. For example, in one famous study, he suggested that madness acquired some of the stigma of leprosy partly because of the chance circumstance that the same buildings which had accommodated leprosy suffers were later used to incarcerate people who were mentally ill (Foucault, 2001). He argued that although the connection was subsequently forgotten, the negative association was transferred from one set of sufferers (lepers) to the other (people with mental illness). It influenced the treatment of the mentally ill and persisted into contemporary thinking, given fortuitously by history yet having important social consequences for social attitudes and practices around mental illness.

This example also illustrates a second premise: such an aggregate of ideas and meanings or, in Foucault's term, 'discursive formation' is a form of knowledge which is inextricably linked to the workings of society. To understand this point in relation to the example mentioned above, consider, first, the difference between the terms 'mad' and 'mentally ill', and second, how the categorization of people as mentally ill inevitably involves a chain of connections. The authority of the experts who can ascribe such categories is linked to a justification for treating supposedly mentally ill people in certain ways, the traditions and institutions which provide the 'knowledge' underpinning the justification and the power structures and institutions through which the treatment is administered. The words and terms used in various contexts, officially and colloquially, are part of the chain; the language is inseparable from the social phenomenon.

The notion of the social world as shaped by historically accrued, partially contingent knowledge and language has further implications. It inverts the commonsense assumption that knowledge, recorded or unrecorded, follows faithfully from the details of the world which pre-exists it, like a description of what 'is'. A classification like 'mad' may even be seen to produce what it purportedly describes (a person different to most others?). This is a challenge to the possibility of objective knowledge and it points to a further premise: people do not necessarily learn by observing. Rather, what they see is largely determined by already existing, socially circulated knowledge. This point undermines the concept of 'truth', changing its status from what 'is' (or was) to what is generally believed and accepted. There can be more than one truth! It also implicates knowledge with power since the workings of the social world will be closely connected to the accepted truths of that world, such as which people 'are' right, or best, or most important, or deserving of reward, and which have the power to dictate or influence the accepted truths. This is discussed further in the section 'Knowledge, Truth and Power'.

This section has indicated one aspect of discourse analysis, that is, the study of language as evidence of a system or formation of meanings and the connections of those meanings to society, including the power relations within society. However, such an analysis can be criticized as static because it maps meanings onto language as if they do not change. This potentially conflicts with two other premises which are particularly relevant to the analysis of talk. The first is that meaning is 'indexical', that is, it depends on and changes with context. A simple example is provided by the reference of a pronoun such as 'her', 'him' or 'it'. The meaning of the pronoun will be given by the surrounding physical environment of objects and people, or by the preceding talk. For example, 'it' may be something which a speaker points to or touches, or something which is not present but has already been made a topic of conversation.

The second premise is that meanings are constituted through what is 'done', that is, through practices and processes. One example would be how information can be made 'official' through processes such as publication or the release of statements. Another would be in talk, the way that a speaker's identity may be indicated not by what is said but by *how* it is said, for example, with authority or obedience. Each of these points opens up further directions for investigation, some of which are illustrated in the studies discussed in Chapter 3. The current chapter continues with a discussion of theories which have contributed to the study of social activities or practices, and in particular, language use and talk as an everyday practice.

## Theorizing language as social practice

A key writer in this tradition is Harold Garfinkel (1917–2011) who developed the sociological field of ethnomethodology. The following short quotation sets out its main points:

> Ethnomethodologists seek to understand how we 'do' social life and how 'the properties of social life which seem objective, factual and transsituational, are actually managed accomplishments or achievements of local processes'. (Zimmerman, 1978, p. 11, quoted in Stokoe, 2003, p. 320)

Ethnomethodology is therefore concerned with the study of practices and processes. In addition, it begins with the study of what is 'local'. It challenges macro-level explanations of social order by explaining the functioning of society as based in micro-level, rule-governed interactions between people. Garfinkel famously encouraged his students to disrupt the order of local situations, for example, by behaving at home as if they were guests rather than members of the family. The purpose was to demonstrate the tacitly understood rules and forms of behaviour which regulate ordinary life practices and become obvious only when they are 'breached'. In this view, as people competently function in each small situation of daily life, drawing on the knowledge and skills they have acquired as members of society, their myriad activities combine to constitute an orderly whole. Society is therefore seen to operate from the 'bottom up', although ethnomethodologists would reject any neat macro–micro hierarchy.

Following from ethnomethodology, talk and spoken interactions can be analysed as orderly social activities. This is the approach of conversation analysis (CA), based on the work of Harvey Sacks (Jefferson, 1992). It is sometimes referred to as a form of discourse analysis and sometimes as a separate field, also known as the study of 'talk in interaction'. Conversation analysts are interested in talk as a social practice and in the meanings which are established within the immediate conversational context. The data they analyse are usually ordinary conversational interactions (often referred to as 'mundane'), such as phone conversations or talk at the dinner table. These are electronically recorded and then transcribed in close detail, for example, to include emphases, pauses, overlapping talk and sometimes other details like intonation. There is a preference for analysing 'naturally occurring talk' which would have taken place whether or not the researcher (or recording equipment) was present, rather than an interview set up for the purposes of the research. This kind of investigation of talk as a social practice potentially (some would say definitely!) conflicts with the analysis of meaning systems which is associated with the tradition discussed in the previous section. Meanings are assumed to be established within the context of the talk, rather than being given by society and then imported into the situation being studied.

An analysis of talk as a social practice also challenges many established ideas about communication and about people themselves. The analyst studies how talk is shaped to the interactional context, to perform functions within that context. To understand this, consider the kind of talk which might be labelled 'apologizing'. This would often be assumed, by people other than ethnomethodologists, to follow on from some prior mental activity: a person feels apologetic or thinks something like 'I was wrong', and then expresses that feeling or thought in talk. As another example, telling a story about something that happened in the past might be assumed to follow from the mental activity of 'remembering'. However, in the practice-focussed logic of ethnomethodology and conversation analysis, apologizing or storytelling talk occurs in response to other talk, as part of a sequence of steps or moves like a social dance. The telling of the story or the apology occurs at the point where it is made appropriate by the ongoing social interaction. It is therefore understandable as part of that interaction. In summary, what a person says can be accounted for only with reference to interactional processes; it is not described or explained in terms of some kind of individual and internal mental or emotional prompt. This view has implications not only for interpretations of language but also for models of people as language users. It has contributed to important debates in psychology, discussed in more detail in the section 'Discourse analysis in psychology'.

A rather different emphasis on talk as an activity, usually associated with the concept of performance, derives from the work of the philosopher J. L. Austin (1911–60). He emphasized the distinction between the label given to an activity and the words used to carry out that activity. Interrupting, for example, may be accomplished using a variety of expressions ('Excuse me', 'Just a minute', 'But'), not to mention non-verbal sounds and actions (clearing the throat, coughing, raising a hand and so on) but it seldom involves the words 'I interrupt'. This may seem a rather obvious point but Austin's work is important for discourse analysts because it draws attention to the functions of language, especially but not exclusively of talk. These functions can be understood only by considering its use in context.

This section and the preceding one have discussed two different theorizations of language and meaning, in terms of systems and practices. Together and separately they challenge many everyday assumptions about language, including how it works for communication. The next section discusses theories of language as communication.

## Theorizing language as communication

Communication between two people can be represented very simply using a three-part model of sender, communication channel and receiver (Wertsch, 1990). A piece of information which originates in the person who is the sender, perhaps as a thought or observation, is conveyed through the channel to the receiver. If the model is elaborated to include language as the channel of communication, the information is first encoded or trans-lated into language by the sender, then decoded or translated again by the receiver. The model implies that the information is communicated without distortion: neither the encoding and decoding processes nor the transmis-sion in language alters its meaning in any way. The communication process functions so efficiently that it can be ignored. This is the assumption which operates when what someone says is assumed to be entirely intelligible as the utterance and intended meaning of that individual speaker.

However, this model can be challenged. The problems with it become obvious if it is applied to the example discussed earlier, that is, if the com-munication channel consists of letters. The model would imply that the meaning of a letter originates entirely in the writer and has no additional meanings which are given by its social context. It would therefore discount any meanings which arise as part of the social practices around language, such as the style of the letter, and it would discount too any indexical meanings belonging to the correspondence or communication *itself*. These might include the kinds of emotion- or affect-laden meanings which develop over an extended communication (such as pet names or special occasions referred to by lovers, or a particular grievance which becomes the charged focus of a dispute between neighbours.) The model would imply, too, that the language of the letter has only one meaning which will not change in different contexts, including different times.

Most, if not all, academic discourse analysts would reject the simple three-part model, as James Wertsch (1990) discusses. The point of presenting it here is to draw attention to this rejection and, in doing so, to indicate some of the interests of academics who study language as communication, particularly sociolinguists. Their 'social view of language' (Kress, 2001, pp. 29–38) can be presented as a rejection of the study of languages as stable, coherent, intact systems of words and grammar which can be understood without reference to the contexts in which they are used, or to the language users themselves. A social study of language would assume that a standard named language, such as English or French, has many different versions and variations. There are the 'dialects' associated with communities defined by geographical location, class, age, multilingualism, among other possibilities. There are the differences in how people use languages in specific contexts and relationships, and for different purposes: these various 'registers' incorporate distinctive vocabulary and grammar (think of the different ways in which children speak to their friends and to their parents or teachers). Most of these variations carry social meanings and values (think of the preferred speaking style for a TV news presenter, or a government spokesperson). Some of the variations are more within the language user's control than others; in a specific situation (the pupil in trouble who is talking to the head teacher) the user will make choices about the language to be used but some variations, such as class and regional dialects, may be relatively inflexible.

The approach known as Critical Discourse Analysis is specifically concerned with the connections between language use and 'dominance' (van Dijk, 1998, pp. 367–93) and the ways in which elite groups use language to exercise power in society. A Critical Discourse Analyst will be interested in how a group influences the kinds of accepted ideas which were referred to in the section 'Theorizing language as systems or aggregates of meanings'. As just one example, those who have access to the media will be in a better position to influence which political arguments are promoted and to establish consensus, even at the level of setting the terms and categories which become taken for granted (as in the example of 'mad' or 'mentally ill') with all the consequences attached to that language.

This short overview suggests further possibilities for the analysis of language use. Looking at a text (a piece of talk or writing or other language use), the analyst might consider the words used and their associations, as discussed in the section'Theorizing language as systems or aggregates of meanings', in connection to the larger social environment, the power structures and relationships within it and also the position and purpose of the particular language user. Features of pronunciation and grammar might mark dialect, such as a regional accent, or indicate the formality related to a particular situation. The analyst might look at the social values attached to variations. In popular entertainment and drama, these have often been invoked as a basis for rather cruel comedy. For example, dialect can be used to indicate the foolishness of a character such as an upper class twit or country bumpkin, or an immigrant who speaks a heavily accented, grammatically non-standard form of English. Characters can be mocked for using register inappropriately, perhaps by being overly formal in an attempt to look important, or overly colloquial in a situation which requires formality. The humour derives both from how the characters normally speak, based in prejudice against certain groups of language users, and from the social ignorance exhibited when characters are unable to adapt their talk appropriately to a situation and purpose. The examples are crude but they indicate some of the power attached to the variations in a language and to language competence. This point is summarized by the sociolinguist Gunther Kress as follows:

> In critical linguistics the social is prior; it is a field of power; and power (and power differences) is the generative principle producing linguistic form and difference. Individuals are located in these fields of power, but the powerful carry the day, and the forms which they produce are the forms which shape the system. (Kress, 2001, p. 36)

## Terminology

The discussion of theories in the previous three sections now makes possible a fuller explanation of the terminology around discourse analysis. Many writers use the term 'a discourse' to refer to the language associated with the kind of system or aggregate of meanings which Foucault calls a 'discursive formation'. For example, a 'discourse of education' might refer to all the terminology, theory and argument associated with education or, more usefully, with one approach to education, such as a child-centred discourse. In some discussions, the term 'discourse' may not be confined to the language but be extended to encompass the relevant language users, the institutions and so on. Stuart Hall summarizes Foucault's notion of a 'discourse' as

> a group of statements which provide a language for talking about – a way of representing the knowledge about – a particular topic a particular historical moment ... Discourse is about the production of knowledge through language. But ... since all social practices entail *meaning*, and meanings shape and influence what we do – our conduct – all practices have a discursive aspect. (Hall, 1992, p. 291)

Understood in this sense, a discourse pre-exists any particular occasion of language use and is available to be drawn on or used selectively, according to the situation and purpose. It is a 'resource' for talk. Analysts may refer to discursive resources or, more generally, cultural resources. Some analysts discuss particular kinds of resources, such as a 'narrative resource' or an 'interpretative repertoire'. Critical discursive psychologists (e.g., Edley and Wetherell, 1995; Wetherell, 1998) have preferred the term 'repertoire' to escape the totality of Foucault's notion of a discourse: for example, in research about masculinity, they would be interested in the multiple and often conflicting repertoires in play, rather than in an overarching discourse of masculinity. Even within a specific tradition like this, the definitions of resources are likely to vary and be reviewed for the purposes of a new study.

Somewhat differently, 'discourse' can refer to the use of language as a practice, and especially to talk. For example, Norman Fairclough, who contributed to the founding of Critical Discourse Analysis, defines 'discourse' as 'language as a form of social practice' (2001b, pp. 229–66). Analysts may refer to the discourse of a user or group of users ('politicians' discourse'), and also to the discourse data which are being analysed.

Following from both these uses, discourse analysis refers to the study and interpretation of multiple aspects of talk or language use, as discussed in the sections 'Theorizing language as social practice' and 'Theorizing language as communication'. However, the issue is complicated because some influential writers have developed their own definitions. For example, the sociolinguist James Gee calls discourses 'social practices' (Gee, 1992, p. 107) and then defines them at greater length as follows:

> Each Discourse in a society is 'owned' and 'operated' by a socio-culturally defined group of people. These people are accepted as

'members' of the Discourse and play various 'roles', give various 'performances', within it. Each Discourse involves ways of talking, acting, interacting, valuing, and believing, as well as the spaces and materials 'props' the group uses to carry out its social practices. Discourses integrate words, acts, values, beliefs, attitudes, social identities, as well as gestures, glances, body positions, and clothes.

Discourses are ways of displaying (through words, actions, values, and beliefs) *membership* in a particular social group or social network (people who associate with each other around a common set of interests, goals, and activities). Being trained (apprenticed) as a linguist meant that I learned to speak, think and act like a linguist and to recognize others when they do so (not just that I learned lots of facts about language and linguistics). So 'being a linguist' is one of the Discourses I have mastered. (p. 107)

This definition does not limit a 'discourse' to language but includes non-linguistic elements ('ways of acting', 'spaces and materials', 'values and beliefs', 'gestures', 'body positions'). It emphasizes practice but also contains the notion of a discourse as a resource which makes available 'ways of talking, acting' and so on, linked to the performance of an identity associated with a group. That membership will raise issues of power and inequality, for instance, around who is or not included.

Discourse analysis can therefore involve the investigation of language, meanings, resources and practices. It may be associated with critical language study, critical linguistics, sociolinguistics, communication studies, pragmatics, semiotic analysis, discursive psychology and, following Foucault's work, studies of governmentality. These various terms and fields will not be explained in detail (an almost limitless task) but the studies discussed in Chapter 3 refer to some of them. The next two sections of this chapter will summarize some concerns shared by discourse analysts working in the different traditions summarized so far.

## Knowledge, truth and power

Discourse analysis is strongly associated with critical research and many of the issues which researchers investigate relate to the status of knowledge or truth claims. The previous sections have presented arguments that language is not a neutral vehicle through which knowledge is conveyed from one person to another, because meanings will be created and changed in the process of communication. Additional meanings accrue historically. Because of this multiplicity, communication always involves selection between alternative words, grammatical forms, registers and so on, with each alternative carrying different meanings. A famous example is that the terms 'terrorist' and 'freedom fighter' might be used to refer to the same person. Clearly those alternatives are linked to different political positions, allegiances and actions, for example, around how the person in question 'should' be treated.

However, many choices are less clear-cut. Michael Billig and others (Billig et al., 1988) have discussed some of the 'ideological dilemmas' around the multiple meanings and contradictory consequences attached to a single notion or situation. These can be illustrated with the example of the nation as, supposedly, a group or community with a common territory and interests. Susan Condor (2011) shows how speakers confront a dilemma around change and continuity in the nation, specifically, whether it is possible to reconcile a positive view of the contemporary, increasingly diverse national community with the narrow shared history which supposedly defines the national character and limits the membership of the nation. Condor's research shows how speakers attempt to resolve the dilemma in order to support diversity *and* the nation.

Obviously multiple accounts of the 'same' phenomenon are possible. 'The nation' is changing *and* stable, diverse and the same, new and old. This kind of inconsistency may appear relatively easy to live with. However, attempts to avoid it in relation to the nation are linked to political ideologies of national purity and historical continuity which continue to be used as a justification for horrendous violence. One concern for discourse analysts is the multiple versions of what is 'known', the contests around them and the power relationships implicated in these contests.

Theorizing multiplicity also brings into question the 'objective' knowledge which is associated with science. In a famous discourse analytic study, two sociologists, Nigel Gilbert and Michael Mulkay (1984), examined scientists' accounts of their experiments. In a conventional view of science, scientists conduct experiments in order to make original discoveries which add to what is already known. The findings can be checked or validated by repeating the experiments and producing the same results. However, Gilbert and Mulkay showed that the scientists' accounts of their work, especially in informal talk, were not consistent with this conventional view. For example, the scientists' talk indicated a practical conflict between using their time to do original work or to replicate experiments. Originality was more highly valued. The scientists would therefore describe themselves as repeating an experiment in a slightly different way, or developing a different explanation for the effect which has been observed; they emphasized their own originality while suggesting that *other* scientists do the less interesting work of exact replication to check previous findings. The point of Gilbert and Mulkay's research is not to discredit the scientists but to show that even in this supposedly 'objective' field, language has contextualized social functions. 'Scientists employ forms of talk which enable them to accomplish both self-validation and the attribution of originality' (Mulkay, 1985, p. 145).

The psychologist Kenneth Gergen criticized the notion of objective knowledge operating within his own discipline (1985) and suggested that social psychologists should not ally themselves with natural scientists or experimental psychologists. He emphasized the importance of language for shaping meaning, arguing that people understand themselves and the world in terms which are 'social artifacts, products of historically situated interchanges among people' (p. 267). He suggested, therefore, that psychologists should study language as part of 'human meaning systems' (p. 270), rather than the world or the mental events which the language might be purported to represent. This is now a principle of discursive psychology, discussed in the section 'Discourse analysis in psychology'.

Many discourse analysts, including those associated with Critical Discourse Analysis, investigate the versions of knowledge which have become accepted as truth (i.e., as if there is no other version) and which advance the interest of particular groups in society. Their interest is partly in the processes through which 'truth' is established. The analysts may look at how language is used to present and perpetuate a version, sometimes referred to as an ideology, so that it comes to be taken for granted, or how persuasive arguments may be advanced. 'If the minds of the dominated can be influenced in such a way that they accept dominance, and act in the interest of the powerful out of their own free will, we use the term *hegemony*' (van Dijk, 1998, p. 372) One issue here will be, of course, who is doing the arguing and how they can make their arguments heard, for instance, because they have access to news media.

Following Foucault, some researchers have explored the origins and implications of taken-for-granted ideas and categorizations. Such research potentially undermines established authority and institutions. It will be useful here to look at the example of the work of Nikolas Rose (1989; 1996) which employs Foucauldian theory as a basis for research on the history of official interventions in family life in the United Kingdom, including those that have taken place through health and educational policies. For example, he investigated how the discourses of education associated with compulsory schooling gave rise to new identities, such as the identity of a bad learner or child with learning difficulties (Rose, 1989). His work indicates that for a bad learner to exist, there needs to be a framework of norms and expectations about good or normal learning. This in turn rests on a set of institutions, an education system, which defines and monitors such learning, and also on a legal system which makes participation in the education system compulsory. It has implications which extend into other areas of life. For instance, the notion of 'good' parenting expands to involve giving attention to a child's educational success, encouraging children to learn to read and so on.

Rose's work is an example of the study of governmentality, of how power works indirectly in contemporary social worlds, often referred to as neo-liberal democratic societies. The argument is that people have come to govern themselves, regulating their own behaviours in order to achieve outcomes (such as successful school careers for their children) which they have learned to believe are desirable. Rose traces the complex processes through which people come to monitor and modify their own behaviours in order to comply with social norms, and the role of knowledge within these processes. He coined a new term, the 'psy disciplines', to refer to psychology and related fields which formulate the knowledge which drives many of these processes.

## Culture and identity

Another important group of concerns for discourse analysts relate to culture and identity. Culture might be defined as the social knowledge which is distinctive to a particular society as a whole, or to groups within it, and is therefore a source of identity. This overlaps with James Gee's definition of a discourse, quoted earlier, which relates a discourse to a group almost as a form of insider knowledge. Extending this idea, the group might be assumed to share a culture or body of knowledge which confers a specific worldview (e.g., think of the different discourses of settlers and indigenous people in a colonized country: see Dixon et al., 1997, for an analysis which considers these). The group might also share discourses as language practices, such as ways of speaking, which mark them as members, to each other and outsiders. These assumptions indicate several possible directions for research, into the discourses which distinguish particular groups and create identities, the ways in which discourse practices are acquired as part of the process of learning and becoming part of the group and the conflicts which different discourse practices may give rise to, for example, when ways of speaking are misunderstood, or prompt discrimination. However, these assumptions also raise a number of issues which new discourse researchers need to consider.

One concerns the boundaries of cultures. It is easy to exaggerate the distinctiveness of the discourse of, for example, women and men, or young people and old. People do not live in neatly bounded, exclusive communities with their own entirely separate languages and social knowledge. They understand each other and, even more importantly, they are members of multiple groups simultaneously, or, to put it another way, they have multiple identities. It is therefore illogical to interpret language use as direct evidence of group membership. For example, when a woman speaks, she may not be speaking *as* a woman, or as a citizen of her country, or as a daughter, or mother, or member of her profession, even though she has a claim to all of those identities and more. In addition, even if she intends to speak as a woman, she is not necessarily representing the view of all women, or national citizens, or whatever. This is a caution against interpreting a participant as the 'voice' of an identity. Discourse analytic studies of identity have employed several alternative approaches, separately or in combination.

One involves the analysis of the shifting identity positions which are taken up in talk. Within the different situations, interactions and relationships which make up people's social lives, they occupy different 'positions', each with an associated point of view and interests (Davies and Harré, 1990). Some positions are conferred by others, as when a person in authority speaks 'as' the authority, thereby positioning another person as a subordinate. Other positions are more actively taken up or claimed by people themselves. Discourse analysts study 'positioning', defined by Bethan Benwell and Elizabeth Stokoe (2006) as 'the process through which speakers adopt, resist and offer "subject positions" that are made available in "master narratives" or "discourses"'(p. 139). As indicated by the references to multiple actions (adopting, resisting, offering), this kind of analysis focuses on practices. It might extend to consider other actions including claiming and contesting. The term 'identity work' is often used to encompass these active negotiations around available and aspired to identities.

Identity may also be discussed and analysed in terms of performance. This concept has been mentioned already with reference to the philosopher J. L. Austin. Austin's work is cited by the feminist philosopher Judith Butler who introduced the notion of gender identities as performance. In other words, she argued for a shift from a conceptualization of *being* a gender to *doing* or performing it, 'though *not* a doing by a subject who might be said to pre-exist the deed' (Butler, 1990, p. 33). In other words, the person does not pre-exist the performance, like an actor playing a part, but is made or constituted through the practice or process of performance. Butler suggests that performance is not a once-and-for-all accomplishment but involves 'a stylized repetition of acts' (p. 179) which constructs someone's gender identity. Butler's primary purpose is political; she is constructing a basis for feminist politics which does not assume that 'women' share a single essential or 'foundationalist' identity (p. 189). Her work is theoretical rather than empirical but the concept of the performance of identity is central to many discourse analyses, including studies of gender. As with ethnomethodology, the focus is therefore on practice, on 'doing' rather than 'being' (a particular kind of person).

A somewhat different discourse analytic focus involves the investigation of the discursive or cultural resources which are associated with a particular identity. These can be considered as setting a range of possibilities for an identity as, for example, a man (Edley and Wetherell, 1995, 1997) or a single woman (Reynolds, 2008). The analysis is usually linked to positioning and the ways in which possible identities are taken up, resisted or otherwise negotiated.

Implicit in all of these accounts is the notion that identities, and social worlds, are emergent. People and their lives do not follow machine-like cycles or repetitions (despite Butler's reference to a stylized repetition). Instead, they are understood to be part of an ever-ongoing flow in which actions and interactions produce novel circumstances and situations. It may be possible to look *back* and trace the pathways which led up to the present, but the future is always uncertain, unfolding or hatching out of the present in unforeseeable ways. People and their lives are always in the making, never finalized or wholly predictable.

## Discourse analysis in psychology

This section is included because although discourse analysis has been widely used across the social sciences, and in related disciplines such as sociolinguistics, education and gender studies, it has a special status in psychology. Many of the key texts on discourse analysis as an empirical approach have been written by social psychologists. In addition, discourse theories have led to the development of a new sub-discipline, discursive psychology. This final section introduces some of the main debates associated with discourse analysis and discursive psychology.

An early and highly influential text, *Discourse and Social Psychology* by Jonathan Potter and Margaret Wetherell, first published in 1987, challenged established quantitative and qualitative methods for researching attitudes and opinions (Potter and Wetherell, 1987). Potter and Wetherell criticized the standard questionnaire design in which the respondent chooses an answer from a scale ('Agree strongly', 'Agree', 'Disagree', etc). They also criticized less structured interviews in which participants are invited to state their opinions on an issue. Their arguments followed from the two broad premises which have already been introduced in this chapter. The first is the assumption that meaning is social, derived from larger discourses or formations rather than reflecting the mental activities of individual speakers. The second is the conceptualization of talk and other communications as orderly social practices, shaped by the communicative situation (e.g., an interview) rather than, again, by the particular individuals who are party to the communication. Following these ideas, Potter and Wetherell rejected the notion of an attitude as somehow fixed and internal to a person, enabling translation into a choice on scale or into a neat statement of opinion. A further premise here is that talk or language (or other representations) cannot be a simple vehicle for an opinion which already exists: the medium inevitably shapes the message, or even creates it.

These arguments, and in many cases Potter and Wetherell's own work, continue to be important for discourse analytic research. They inform investigations of communication and the situated meanings which are constructed, and co-constructed, within the immediate context of an interaction (such as a conversation) and the action of communicating. Following these arguments, many discourse analysts avoid treating talk as evidence of the fixed opinion or thought processes of individuals. This distinguishes their work from most other social research. Instead, they analyse either groups of meanings as discursive resources (as already noted, these can be labelled in different ways, for example, as 'discourses' or 'interpretative repertoires') or else the social practices through which meaning is constituted, especially the social practices of talk. Many analyses combine these foci.

Potter and Wetherell's work has also made an important contribution to ongoing discussion, within psychology and in the social sciences more generally, about the nature of the person and, relatedly, about identity ('who I am'). This discussion generally rejects what might be called a commonsense theory of the speaker or language user, that is, as an individual container for an internal mental and emotional machinery which emits or expresses outputs into the social world. One project for discursive psychologists has been to re-interpret 'mental' processes as social activities. By considering, say, remembering as a kind of talk rather than as the expression of a cognitive process, discursive psychologists have challenged established theories and understandings of the person.

Discursive approaches also tend to challenge our sense of ourselves as free agents. One contrasting theory is of the person, or subject, as subordinate (or 'subjected') to the workings of power in society. This suggests that the position which a person occupies within the power and knowledge systems discussed by Foucauldian scholars (a 'subject position') determines who he or she is. Identity is therefore given by external circumstances and situations rather than internal aspects of an individual. Nikolas Rose's work, mentioned earlier in this chapter, explores this making or 'subjectification' as a complex and extended process (1989; 1996). In his words, subjectification involves 'apparatuses, practices, machinations, and assemblages' including aspects of organizational and institutional life. He suggests that the process produces an illusion of freedom and agency. People learn to discipline themselves to act in certain ways yet believe that they are freely choosing to do so. As noted previously, Rose has explored the subjectification associated with education together with the resulting forms of behaviour and monitoring through which, as he describes it, people 'govern' themselves. In a more recent example of research which employs similar concepts, Rosalind Gill (2008), analysing advertisements, has discussed the sexual subjectification by which an identity for a young woman as agentic or empowered is tied to certain demanding require- ments, to be 'beautiful ... sexy, sexually knowledgeable/practised and always "up for it"' (p. 35).

A different theory of identity and the subject is associated with social constructionism and (some areas of) discursive psychology. This is the concept of a distributed self, originally proposed by Jerome Bruner (1990). The underlying argument is that people are inseparable from the contexts in which they function, including the contexts of their relationships with others. Visually, this might be represented as a shift from a neat diagram of a person as contained within the outline of the body, to multiple images of the same person in different situations, all superimposed on each other, with the outline of the body blurring into the different backgrounds. The implications for psychology are that the cognitive processes associated with the container model of the person are re-interpreted as occurring across the whole range of social practices which make up a person's life. An example of how this might occur was indicated in the earlier discussion of 'remembering' and 'telling a story'. As one writer summarizes it, in this view the mind is 'immanent in dis- course practices' (Herman, 2007, p. 308), 'spread out as a distributional flow in what participants say and do' (p. 312) and located in all of their 'socio-communicative activities unfolding within richly material settings' (p. 308). This striking idea has been hailed as part of a 'second cognitive revolution' (Harré and Gillett, 1994) because it assumes that 'discursive phenomena, for example, acts of remembering, are not manifestations of hidden subjective, psychological phenomena' (p. 27). It can be linked to classic observational empirical studies of work which investigate the combined functioning and capacities of a technological system and the worker within it, as a single unit (e.g., Goodwin, 1994). There are similarities, and some direction connections, to research in the areas of distributed cognition and Actor Network Theory.

Discursive psychological theories of talk as a social practice generally assume that the person is active and to some extent operating independ- ently or agentically, rather than following the dictates of the larger situa- tion or society. As already outlined, a speaker is assumed to be positioned by others and by society as having a certain identity, but also actively to position her or himself, for example, by choosing between available subject positions (in talk); in other words, identities are assumed to some extent conferred and to some extent actively claimed and contested. This is a key assumption in critical discursive psychology (e.g., Wetherell, 1998; Edley, 2001; Seymour-Smith, 2008).

Working from a different theoretical position, the social psychologist Wendy Hollway has criticized the concept of the subject position as inadequate (Hollway, 1998). She notes that people occupy many different subject positions, yet the identities which these make available do not carry equal importance. Some additional explanation is needed for the emotions attached to some subject positions. Bringing together discourse and psychoanalytic theories, she explains this in terms of 'investment'. Some discourse analysts discuss this issue in different terms. For example, in a narrative analysis it can be interpreted as a question of continuity and why some identities persist beyond an immediate, transient situation (see Taylor 2010). An additional point to note here is that in psychoanalytic theory the term 'subject' is associated with a sense of self and a subjective (i.e., not objective) view of the world, in contrast to the notion of people as 'subjects' because people are shaped by or 'subjected to' the workings of power in society. The work of Hollway, with Tony Jefferson, has contributed to a psychosocial research approach (Hollway and Jefferson, 2000).

There is no agreement on a resolution to these various problems around a theorization of identity or the subject in discourse theory. However, discursive approaches may be brought together with other theories, as in Hollway and Jefferson's work. As another example, the self-actualizing identity project proposed by theorists of reflexive modernization, such as Anthony Giddens, can be understood and explored in discursive terms (see Reynolds et al., 2007). The original theory proposes that in contemporary or late modern Western societies, a process of individualization operates through which each person shapes 'who I am' as their own ongoing and reflexive identity project. A discursive psychologist approach draws out the multiple possibilities and also the conflicts and constraints and negotiations involved in the process of identification. A further example is the work of Scharff (2008; 2011) which variously brings together discursive psychology with ethnomethodology, and with performativity and affect theory.

## Conclusion

This chapter has discussed a wide range of ideas in order to provide an overview of the main theories and issues associated with the field of discourse analysis. It is therefore not possible to produce a unified summary, and nor would it be especially appropriate since discourse analysts do not agree on every point or follow a single composite approach. Nonetheless, for the purposes of the book, it will be useful to expand the definition given at the end of Chapter 1, as follows: *Discourse research involves the analysis of language data as evidence of social phenomena, theorizing language as communication, practice or selective constructions derived from accrued social meanings.*

## Summary

Chapter 2 has introduced some of the theories and issues which shape different approaches to discourse analysis.

# 3 Four examples of discourse analysis

The previous chapters have discussed discourse analysis in general terms. This chapter becomes more specific, looking at four published examples of social research to show how discourse analysis is used by researchers. The examples are journal articles which have been chosen to encompass a variety of projects, problems, forms of data, analytic approaches, theoretical traditions and disciplines. All four fall under the broad umbrella of discourse analysis as it is defined in this book. Some of the researchers use that exact term to describe their work, while others refer to discursive practices and constructions, and the analysis of rhetoric, ideological dilemmas and categorization, following some of the theoretical traditions discussed in Chapter 2.

The account of each article begins with an outline of the research project. It sets out the substantive area and problem being addressed and discusses the major claims or findings. It also describes the data collection and analysis and discusses the analytic concepts which are employed and some important premises of the research. Of course any single study will never be a sufficient model for future research but each of the studies discussed in this section does provide a useful illustration of how a researcher used discourse analysis in empirical work. Readers who are interested in finding out more about the research studies may want to refer back to the original article and to other work by the same academics, although the summaries below do provide enough detail for the introductory purpose of this book.

## Discourses of health and illness

### Example 1

> Kirsten Bell (2010), 'Cancer survivorship, mor(t)ality and lifestyle discourses on cancer prevention', Sociology of Health and Illness 32(3): 349–64.

The first article has been chosen as an example of discourse research on health and illness. It is also a discourse analytic project which combines different methods of data collection, interviewing and observation and different forms of data, including transcribed talk and the researchers' fieldnotes. Another point of interest is that the data were originally collected in two different languages.

Discourse research on health and illness presents an interesting challenge to 'commonsense' in that these are being considered as social rather than straightforward biological issues. The author of the article, Kirsten Bell, conducted an ethnographic study with people who were attending support groups after being diagnosed with cancer. The research has obvious applications, for example, in a medical support context, but it is primarily a sociological study.

Bell's interest was in how cancer patients and cancer survivors engage with lifestyle discourses about 'the importance of lifestyle factors (particularly excess body weight, a poor diet and a sedentary lifestyle) in contributing to cancer and their role in managing disease recurrence or progression' (p. 351). These lifestyle discourses can be found in scientific, medical and health sources ('scientific literature', p. 349; 'public health and health promotion discourses', p. 350). In another version, they are part of 'complementary and alternative medical therapies' (CAM) (p. 350). The discourses will be recognizable to most people: they can be regarded as part of commonsense or shared cultural knowledge, not only in Canada where the research was conducted but also in similar affluent Western societies. In addition, Bell notes that people who attend support groups have been found to develop 'collective understandings' (p. 351) so that these discourses may be regarded as part of the more local knowledge or culture of the groups themselves.

To conduct the research, Bell attended three cancer support groups for English-speaking people with different cancers and also interviewed some of the group members individually. A second researcher on the project attended a group conducted in another language, Cantonese, and conducted interviews with some of its members. Because the researchers were participant-observers in the groups, this is described as 'ethnographic' fieldwork. The inclusion of the Cantonese speakers was intended to capture evidence of cultural variation, with issues this might raise. One example which Bell found was that advice on nutrition and diet in some respects conflicted with 'Chinese dietary practices' (p. 356).

The research project combined three kinds of formal data. The first was the researchers' field notes, which were collected over quite an extended period (eight months) of their attending the support groups. The second was the transcripts from the recorded interviews, and the third the written notes from the interviews. The extracts presented in the article are obviously a very small part of the data. For the project as a whole, Bell analyses field notes from eight months of observations by two researchers, and also the recordings, transcripts and additional notes from the individual interviews. Some of this material would have existed in duplicate, in the original Chinese and an English translation. In addition, Bell refers to medical literature and other background material which provided relevant background to her analysis, including many other studies from both medical and social research traditions. Bell used a software package to manage her data. She notes that this was used only in the initial stages of coding, presumably to organize the data into codes or broad categories.

The article includes extracts from transcripts and also from field notes, as in the following example:

> Sandra volunteers that in her own case she thinks that it [the cause of her cancer] was genetics but admits that it may also be due to the fact that she was overweight. Daphne expresses surprise at this [Sandra is on palliative chemotherapy and has lost a considerable amount of weight since her diagnosis with metastatic cancer] and Sandra responds, 'Oh, you should have seen me, I was a real porker!' She then looks down at her stomach and sighs that she is still overweight – pinching her gut with her fingers to demonstrate her point. (p. 353)

This account is written by Bell and includes background information, about Sandra's therapy and weight loss, which Bell has presumably collected in an interview or through attending previous meetings. The field notes describe an incident with details which indicate that they are the researcher's interpretation and summary. For example, the expression 'a *considerable* amount of weight' (emphasis added) indicates a value judgement and the descriptions that Sandra 'volunteers' and Daphne 'expresses surprise' indicate not only what these participants did (they spoke) but also the researcher's interpretation of their feelings. The field notes are fairly full and were almost certainly based on a combination of rough notes taken during the meeting and the researcher's memory of what happened;

ethnographic researchers typically write up their field notes as soon as possible after observing a situation. As the extract indicates, Bell is using as evidence not only the words but also the feelings and actions of her participants. This contrasts with some other discourse approaches which retain a strict focus on the words used (see Example 3, by Elizabeth Stokoe, in this chapter).

The discourses which Bell discusses are ones that she has found in her larger data set and labelled, sometimes following on from previous researchers who had identified similar patterns or features (the analysis presented in Example 2 in this chapter, by Jovan Byford, similarly builds on the findings of previous research). However, other analysts might focus on different divisions and use different labels. For example, it might seem obvious that discourses of CAM are different to scientific medical discourses, but for Bell's research the more important point is that both reinforce lifestyle discourses. The discourses also reflect the analyst's rather than the participants' interpretation; Bell's participants would not necessarily divide or label the discourses in the same way or even be aware of them.

The lifestyle discourses discussed by Bell link disease management, survival and (continuing) remission to certain behaviours and ways of living, such as eating healthily and doing sufficient exercise. The discourses therefore attribute cancer, at least partly, to a patient's failure to take sufficient care of her or himself. By implication, they potentially position patients negatively, as to blame for their own diseases. Bell herself does not make a judgement about the importance of lifestyle factors in preventing cancer or cancer recurrence. Her interest was in how the people who attended the support groups responded to lifestyle discourses.

The analysis explores the participants' 'complex and ambivalent engagement' (p. 349) with the lifestyle discourses. Bell notes that the discourses are not straightforwardly accepted. Instead, the participants sometimes resist and sometimes selectively take up the advice implicated with the discourses. For example, Bell observed that the people who attended the support groups sometimes made jokes about the advice they received from visiting speakers who advised them on nutrition. However, they would also talk in terms of lifestyle factors when they described steps that they themselves were taking to prevent recurrence of their cancer, such as eating carefully or going to the gym. Bell also notes some gender variation in how these discourses were taken up, with women more likely to refer to advice on diet and the importance of nutrition, and men more likely to discuss exercise. She also notes that there was some resistance through alternative discourses. For example, she cites a participant who suggests that eating what you like is part of a decision to enjoy living in the moment; she is countering a lifestyle discourse with another discourse which might be called 'living life to the full' (although Bell does not use that label).

Lifestyle discourses are individualistic in that they present health as the responsibility of the individual person, in contrast, say, to environmental discourses which might link cancer to problems on a larger social or geographical scale, such as pollution. The lifestyle discourses also link health advice to morality, to notions of being 'good' or 'bad', and to prescriptions about how people should discipline themselves to behave: it is noticeable that the advice tends to present healthy options as ones which people are likely to find less attractive than the unhealthy ones. Bell connects the lifestyle discourses to processes of subjectification, discussing how the discourses position people as certain kinds of subject, that is, as citizens who carry responsibility for their own health and illness. Following the work of Nikolas Rose, discussed in Chapter 2, this research is in the Foucauldian tradition and develops the concept of the self-governing, self-policing 'neoliberal subject'. Bell associates lifestyle discourses with 'Neo-liberal rationality (which) emphasizes the entrepreneurial individual who is called upon to enter into his or her own self-governance' (p. 350). Following from this 'rationality', there is a potential implication that people who become ill are bad citizens because they have brought the illness on themselves by not managing their lives properly. Bell suggests that the patients who are her participants are to some extent aware of being positioned as responsible for becoming ill. She describes this implication and discusses how they variously accept and resist this positioning. She describes how they talk about 'the sense of guilt, blame and judgement that such discourses produced' (p. 360), and also how they resist these discourses by drawing on alternative explanations which would not make the illness their own responsibility, such as genetic or environmental causes of cancer.

Social researchers who are not discourse analysts often approach participants as informants on their own experiences and feelings and opinions, using talk collected in interviews and focus groups. A discourse analytic study like Bell's similarly treats the talk and the researchers' observations as straightforward reporting. Its distinctive feature is the additional analytic concepts it employs, such as 'discourses' and 'governance'. Unlike many discourse analysts, Bell is not particularly interested in the exact words used by participants or the details of their interactions. She employs the concepts of 'a discourse' and 'governance' as operating in meanings and behaviours above or beyond the level of talk.

### Learning from this example

The article by Kirsten Bell presents an example of the following:

- a discourse analytic study of health and illness;
- an analysis of discourses which refers to the work of Foucault, linked to the work of another theorist, Nikolas Rose, and the discussion of governance or governmentality;
- a project which combines discourse analysis and ethnography;
- a relatively large-scale research study involving more than one researcher;
- discourse analysis of several forms of data in combination;
- a research problem or focus which was not the starting point for the project but emerged in the fieldwork, partly as a result of the researchers' observations and partly because the participants themselves referred to it (this kind of emergent focus is typical of both ethnographic and discourse analytic research);
- an analysis which treats talk as a report of participants' feelings and experiences;
- an analysis which approaches participants as active, in sometimes resisting dominant or hegemonic discourses, and also sometimes inconsistent. This is a complex picture.

## The construction of prejudice

### Example 2

> *Jovan Byford (2006), 'Distinguishing "anti-Judaism" from "anti-semitism": Recent championing of Serbian Bishop Nikolaj Velimirović',* Religion, State & Society 34(1): 7–31.

This second article has been chosen as an example of interdisciplinary research which brings together history, political science and social psychology. It is also an example of discourse analysis conducted across two languages. The project presented in the article is part of a long tradition of discourse analytic research into prejudice and racism. There is now a significant body of findings on forms of talk and argument through which social inequalities are rationalized and perpetuated. Researchers have investigated the contemporary language and language practices which attach a negative value to certain groups or categories of people. For example, in a study of 'white' New Zealanders talking about indigenous (Maori) New Zealanders, Wetherell and Potter (1992) noted how talk about 'culture' could be used instead of direct references to 'race'. The central argument of such discourse analytic research is that these new formulations exclude people without violating contemporary social taboos against the open expression of prejudice. In other words, these kinds of talk and writing function as negatively as the more explicit 'biased, prejudiced and racist' talk which is now seen as 'inconsistent with the general values of tolerance' (van Dijk, 1992, p. 115).

Discourse analysts have also explored the kind of political rhetoric which attempts to redefine the nation in order to exclude a negatively valued group. This may be done by constructing a version of history which appears to justify the exclusion, for example, through reference to past conflicts, or by associating an authentic national identity with only a limited part of the current national population. Such rhetoric is part of the ongoing exercise of power in society, inextricably linked to domination, exclusion and sometimes violent oppression. The article analyses an example, looking at details such as how people are categorized and valued, the justifications for the valuing and the construction of arguments and national histories. A central premise of research of this kind is that what is real or 'true' cannot be separated out from the many ways it can be, and is, described. This is not a denial that there is an objective world 'out there' but an assumption that such a world is always viewed and interpreted from a particular perspective and set of interests. There are multiple versions of reality. Observers, including researchers, are insiders with a partial view. Discourse analysts do not try to check the truth of any version or claim but try to understand how it is constructed. By showing that it *is* a construction and interpretation, they therefore open an apparently authoritative and 'truthful' claim to contestation.

The focus of Byford's research is contemporary accounts of a historical figure which potentially function as exclusionary rhetoric against a racially defined group (Jewish people). The article introduces Bishop Nikolaj Velimirović (1880–1956), who is venerated as a spiritual leader, religious philosopher and theologian. He is respected both within the Serbian

Orthodox Church and in Serbian nationalist political circles. He was canonized by the church (i.e., officially named as a saint) in 2003. What makes this an interesting case, from the perspective of research on prejudice, is that the veneration of the bishop persists in contemporary Serbia in spite of a number of controversies surrounding his personal biography, the most important of which is that he was virulently anti-Semitic. The project looked in detail at the various discursive and rhetorical strategies that Velimirović's supporters (both from within the church and outside it) use to avoid the controversy, deny that the bishop was anti-Semitic or in some instances even excuse his stance towards Jews.

Byford's project is a case study, focusing on a specific situation and context but making claims which have a wider importance and application. First, he discusses the national context, Serbia, as an example of an Eastern European nation-state which is in transition from communism and a possible site of the rise of the politics of the far right, in a revival of the fascist movements of the period before World War II. The case is therefore located within the larger scale of historical and political change. Second, he discusses the rhetoric around this case as examples of patterns of argument, justification and denial which have been employed more widely, both in racist and prejudiced talk in more local contexts (the concern of many social psychologists who analyse discourse, as noted above) and in academic and political arguments around anti-Semitism, the particular form of racism which is invoked in the case.

The data for the study were all collected in a relatively short period of four months, centred on a point of celebration of the key figure, Bishop Velimirović. The main data are audio recordings of interviews or 'conversations' between the researcher and 12 Serbian public figures, conducted in July and August 2003, shortly after the bishop was canonized. An unusual feature of the research is that these participants are not anonymized; they are identified 'by name, rank and occupation' on the grounds that they are all public figures. However, they are not discussed as individuals but for their status as influential 'memory-makers' and contributors to political debate.

Another form of data is published and broadcast material in the public domain. Byford analyses a range of texts ('newspaper interviews, commentaries, editorials, serialized texts, debates and readers' letters as well as a small amount of radio material') which had been produced in the preceding months (May and June 2003). The project therefore combines collected and 'found' data consisting of both spoken and written language.

The analysis draws on the researcher's knowledge of the context, including its recent history. The original data are in Serbian and most of the analysis was conducted in that language (the researcher is bilingual). The article is in English and data extracts are presented in translation but sometimes also with the original Serbian, for example, when details of wording or grammar in that language are relevant.

Part of Byford's analytic approach is to examine his data for features of talk and argument ('rhetoric') which have been noted by previous analysts. For example, he shows how some speakers set up a contrast between an extreme position and a supposedly more moderate and, by implication, excusable claim. One common strategy involves creating the distinction between 'real' anti-Semitism (of the kind propagated by the Nazis), and 'biblical' anti-Semitism (a 'critique' of Jews found in parts of the Christian Bible, including the allegation that Jews killed Christ) with the latter being presented as acceptable. By scrutinizing the rhetoric of Velimirović's supporters, and situating it in the appropriate historical and ideological context, the research suggests that the distinction between the two sup-posedly different forms of anti-Semitism is in fact false.

Why is this important? Because, Byford argues, 'this exercise in the redrawing of the boundaries of antisemitism can play an important role in the denial of prejudice' (p. 17). The insistence that there is an 'accept-able' form of anti-Semitism helps to perpetuate anti-Jewish prejudice by presenting it as an acceptable and inevitable aspect of the Christian faith. Like the references to 'culture' studied by Wetherell and Potter (1992), the arguments employed by Velimirović's supporters are a contemporary form of prejudiced talk. Such talk can make negative categorizations of a group appear excusable, unproblematic and, potentially, normal, acceptable and justified, with all that can follow from that. Byford notes that there are 'increasing antisemitic incidents in Serbia' and suggests that the contem-porary celebration of Velimirović is 'the most powerful ideological source of anti-Jewish prejudice in Serbian culture from which contemporary antisemitism derives much of its legitimacy and authority' (p. 27).

This is therefore a wide-ranging study which refers to social, political and intellectual activities taking place over an extended historical period. It traces connections between political and religious ideas, political pur-poses and activities and the talk and writing of specific individuals, such as politicians and journalists. It illustrates the possibilities of a complex 'multi-layered' analysis of broadcast talk and political publications within national and institutional contexts, including the context of the Orthodox Christian church. It also moves between different levels of data, linking 'micro' details of talk and written language (the use of particular words like 'just'); larger discourses of religion and nation; contemporary and historic identities, including both group and individual identities, and 'macro' accounts of history and politics. The analysis builds on a theorization of the working of power in society by which competing claims to authority, entitlement and even social presence are assumed to be played out in talk and argument, sometimes as the justification for other actions. Byford investigates anti-Semitism as a 'lived ideology' (a concept he takes from Billig et al., 1988), that is, as the power relations which are in an ongoing state of renegotiation, contest and reinforcement within the everyday activities and communications of the people who make up society. Byford's interest is in the anti-Semitism which is 'regularly disseminated in speeches, books, articles, sermons and everyday talk' about this figure, Bishop Velimirović.

### Learning from this example

The article by Jovan Byford presents an example of the following:

- a discourse analytic study of prejudice and racism;
- a cross-disciplinary study (politics, history, social psychology);
- an analysis of the discourse of politicians and public figures;
- a case study centred on an event celebrating a particular figure;
- a study which combines analyses on different levels, investigating the intersections of argument and rhetoric with political ideologies, nation-making and the rewriting of history;
- an analysis of racist political rhetoric which links the celebration of a single controversial politicized figure with larger political movements and historical trends;
- a research project which combines collected and 'found' discourse data.

## Gender in talk

### Example 3

> Elizabeth H. Stokoe (2003), 'Mothers, single women and sluts: Gender, morality and membership categorization in neighbour disputes', *Feminism & Psychology* 13(3): 317–44.

The third article presents analyses of talk about disputes between neighbours. It is an example of discourse research which looks at a social problem and also contributes to a major area of social science research, on gender. It is a piece of feminist discursive research in which gender identities are considered as 'performances, constructions and enactments, rather than rigid and unchanging essences' (p. 318). This is consistent with the theories of social practice and identity discussed in Chapter 2, including the work of Judith Butler. In addition, Stokoe's article is an example of research from discursive psychology which presents fine-grained discourse analysis in the conversation analytic tradition, examining the details of interaction and, in particular, categorization.

The starting point for the project which Stokoe discusses is the relationships between neighbours. This topic links the research to the particular social and cultural context of the United Kingdom, since one element is the conventions around how neighbours behave. However (as with Bell's study), similarities can be assumed in many other countries, giving the research a wider relevance and potential application. In addition, as already noted, the research concerns gender. In the opening sections of the article, Stokoe makes connections between these various foci. She argues that 'as neighbours describe, report and account for their own and others' activities, they display the social order, which, in turn, regulates everyday neighbouring practices' (p. 319). In their talk, speakers refer to 'people's actions as either appropriate to or as breaches of the moral or social order' (p. 319), and in doing this, Stokoe notes, they refer to values, to "good' or 'bad' neighbours, women and men' (p. 320). This value-laden talk can partly be taken as evidence of the existing social order, a snapshot of society and its beliefs.

These premises follow from the ethnomethodological tradition. As discussed in Chapter 2, the major premises of ethnomethodology are that society is never static but always in the process of being made and re-made, and sometimes subtly altered, through the ongoing practices of everyday life. The 'macro-level' of society is inseparable from these 'micro-level' practices. Stokoe is considering talk as one such micro-level practice, looking at its effects and consequences. She explores connections between 'neighbour relationships, gender and morality' (p. 317) through an analysis of how women are categorized in the talk, the positive and negative values which are invoked in these categorizations (e.g., around being a good or bad mother) and how the talk functions as part of the ongoing 'constitutions of the gendered social and moral order' (p. 340).

More specifically, the analysis draws on the work of Harvey Sacks, the originator of the approach known as Conversation Analysis (CA). Stokoe uses a variant of CA called Membership Categorization Analysis (MCA). This investigates how talk functions partly through the kinds of grouped or associated meanings which were discussed in Chapter 2. MCA does not refer to discourses but to 'categories [which] may be hearably linked together by native speakers of a culture' (Stokoe, 2003, p. 321). Stokoe cites a famous example from Sacks' work: when we hear "The baby cried. The mommy picked it up', we will of course assume that the 'mommy' is the 'mommy' of the 'baby'. This is because our cultural knowledge of the larger category of 'family' (a Membership Categorization Device) links the categories 'mommy' and 'baby' with certain actions ('category-bound activities') and characteristics ('natural predicates'). MCA explores how a brief reference to one part of the MCD may invoke other parts, ideas of what is normal and so on.

Like CA, this can be seen as a 'technical' approach (Schegloff, 1997) in that it begins with a close examination of what the participants say and builds up an interpretation and argument from the details of their talk, in this case, about good and bad neighbour behaviour by women and men. However, it also draws on the analyst's own insider knowledge as a member of society since she explores the 'inferences' derived from the social context in which the language is being used, that is, the wider social meanings of categories, as well as the meanings which come out of the immediate conversation.

It is important not to assume that Stokoe is interpreting her speakers as planning their talk in advance, like master strategists. In the approach she uses, talk is understood as part of living, that is, as a form of action which, like body movements (walking, gesturing, changing facial expressions) carries meanings for (most) people around us, is more or less ongoing, and is *done* mostly without thinking or preparation. As someone interested in the working of the physical body might slow a film to study the details of the movements of limbs and muscles, so analysts like Stokoe use audio recordings of talk, transcribed in great detail, in order to examine how conversation is 'done'. This is therefore very different from an unravelling of the intended implications of a pre-planned statement, like a political speech or a public relations release. A study like Byford's which uses the latter forms of data might assume that speakers are presenting well-rehearsed arguments which perhaps were planned and carefully worded in advance;

however, as discourse analysis this will still assume that the talk is an action which occurs in context and is shaped by that context. It will be a unique situated version, even if to some extent it repeats arguments and wording which have been prepared and used before.

Stokoe's study uses two forms of data. One consists of televised recordings in which people talk to chat show hosts about problem neighbours. The other is recordings from centres in which mediators attempt to resolve disputes between neighbours by talking to the people involved. As in most conversation analytic studies, Stokoe's recordings are transcribed in close detail to show the irregularities of ordinary talk: repetition and re-starts; sounds which are not words ('mmm', 'hhh'); pauses; overlaps between the talk of different speakers; and some features of *how* the words are spoken (e.g., more or less quickly and more or less loudly).

This is one of the data extracts presented in the article. It is part of the talk from a mediation session in which people are talking about a neighbour with whom they have a dispute:

1   E: [I mean I came home the other day and she was (.) a:rguing with
2   somebody at the top of her voice in the street (.) [and it was eff'ing
3   ? [(?)
4   E: this and [eff'ing that
5   L: [yeah (.) she's eff'ing all the time=
6   E: and I can't beli↑e::ve that somebody would have such a showdown in the
7   street=
8   G: =have you heard her shouting at the kids why don't you piss off? to
9   these tiny little kids (.) at the gate? (.) I've heard her saying it
10  (.) you know (.) this I don't know [. . .]
11  C: is she has anybody actually approached her
12  L: she [( )
13  E: [how can she [( )
14  G: [how can you ↑talk to the woman?
15  L: you just get a mouthful

Following the principles of MCA, Stokoe's analysis of this talk considers the categories of people involved and the activities which are linked to these categories. In this extract, she notes that 'the category 'woman' is linked to activities including 'arguing', 'eff'ing', 'shouting at the kids' and saying 'why don't you piss off' (p. 340). To understand the significance of this link between category and activity, think about the different meanings which would be invoked if the same activities were linked to another, male category of person, such as 'man' or 'youth'. As Stokoe notes, there are 'moral' issues being invoked in this account: 'Here, "bad" women swear in the street and in front of children, they are foul-mouthed, they argue in public places and are bullies.' The account of their neighbour which these speakers build up is not only 'about' a particular incident but also about wider social values and expectations regarding women, their roles and behaviours. Stokoe comments: 'In constructing such categorizations, the participants display their category knowledge (e.g., "women" should not "swear") and position themselves as powerful knowers of the "right" way for women to act (Nilan, 1995).' In short: 'Neighbour disputes about noise, vandalism and communal spaces are enmeshed with moral assessments about appropriate behaviours for women' (p. 340).

Stokoe is interested in the gendered nature of the neighbours' complaints for several reasons. First, as she comments, they probably reflect the continuing cultural association of women with home, local neighbourhoods and 'community and domestic space'. Second, they show how 'women' and their inappropriate activities become the focus of neighbour disputes' (p. 332). She suggests that this is a form of 'cultural regulation' because the disputes function to reinforce established meanings around gender and gender identities: 'in order to maintain "viable" femininity, women must engage only in those activities conventionally associated with their category.' The disputes about the proper behaviour of neighbours are therefore also about the proper behaviour of women more generally, and the policing of one, in the broad sense of watching and attempting to control, is part of the social policing of the other. In the terms used in this book, gendered discourses are reinforced. A third claim which Stokoe is making is that this analysis of how gender is invoked in one kind of dispute, between neighbours, is likely to be relevant to other situations since gender is almost always present as a potential point for comment: it is 'a pervasive resource'.

In her more recent work, Stokoe (2010) has extended the concept of MCDs in an analysis of the talk of men who are being interviewed by the police. There is a strong pattern of the suspects categorizing themselves in a certain way, as the kind of men who do not hit women. This is not just a matter of self-description; the categorization functions as a denial that they have committed an offence. Stokoe is arguing against the kind of interview-based research which treats a discourse as a generalized resource drawn on to talk *about* something. By showing a much more specifically situated use of categorization to *do* something, and do something 'consequential' for the speaker, Stokoe emphasizes the functional nature of talk in interactional contexts.

### Learning from this example

This article by Elizabeth Stokoe presents an example of the following:

- a discourse analytic study of gender;
- a discourse analytic study of a social problem with findings which have practical applications (Stokoe's website provides further details of her involvement in related work);
- Membership Categorization Analysis, a form of conversation analysis;
- an analysis which emphasizes the functional nature of talk;
- a project which uses naturally occurring data;
- a project which combines found data and newly collected data;
- an analysis with a focus which emerged from the data (an important principle in conversation analytic research); the research was not set up as a project about gender;
- an analysis of closely transcribed talk which avoids any interpretation in terms of the speakers' intentions, motives, emotions or other 'inner states'.

## Leadership in an organization

### Example 4

> *Ruth Wodak, Winston Kwon and Ian Clarke* (2011), *'"Getting people on board": Discursive leadership for consensus building in team meetings'*, Discourse & Society 22(5): 592–644.

The fourth article discusses discourse analytic research in the area of workplace and organization studies. In the words of the authors and researchers, the research adopts 'an interdisciplinary discourse-oriented approach to leadership in meetings and teams, studying discourse in use' (p. 593). It investigates how leadership is 'accomplished' or 'performed' in the chairing of workplace meetings, particularly the skills and 'strategies' employed (p. 594). The article suggests that this approach contrasts with previous writing and theorizing in which leadership is discussed either as a style of setting goals and giving rewards (transactional leadership), or in terms of the leader providing a role model (transformational leadership). The research project is therefore presented as a novel investigation of an established topic. The research is described as 'critical', first because of this challenge to established understandings of leadership, and second because of its concern with the links between leadership and power.

The article sets out its rationale for adopting a discursive approach to the study of leadership. The premises are that the effectiveness of a team depends on shared agreement, or consensus, among its members, and the formation of such consensus depends on good leadership. Within an organization, the people officially designated as leaders are potentially powerful, but not all of them will fulfil this potential. The successful performance or enactment of leadership requires 'discursive skills' and strategies and these can be investigated through an analysis of the talk which occurs in meetings, although the full context of this talk needs to be understood.

The research was conducted in an Australian company, referred to pseudonymously as Defence Systems International (DSI). Two field researchers observed meetings and other group interactions (workshops, an away day) over a six-month period, making field notes. They also conducted individual interviews with some of the staff who attended the meetings. The data set consists of the transcripts from 150 hours of recordings of the meetings and interviews, although at some stages of the analysis a further selection is made. The interpretation and discussion of the transcripts is informed by the background knowledge which the researchers obtained from the fieldwork. This is referred to in their accounts of the participants, the issues under discussion, the influence of people not present and subsequent events. The ethnographic element of the research is therefore used to locate the meeting transcripts within the larger context of the company.

The project combines this ethnographic element with Critical Discourse Analysis (CDA). CDA refers to a family of approaches rather than a single method (Wodak, 2007). It is interdisciplinary, drawing on sociology and sociolinguistics, and explores language as an element of social processes by considering a range of features or aspects. Critical Discourse Analysts study interactions and sequences of talk, like conversation analysis researchers such as Elizabeth Stokoe, and they are also interested in the argumentative and rhetorical aspects of talk and texts, like those which are the focus of Jovan Byford's study. Critical Discourse Analysts also investigate the kinds of patterns which Kirsten Bell and others call discourses (see Fairclough, 2001b, pp. 229–66). More distinctively, CDA involves a micro-analysis of details of grammatical and communicative ('pragmatic') aspects of talk including, in this study, pronouns and tenses, and speech acts, such as questioning and telling.

The discourse analytic approach adopted in the study is described in detail. The data set of the transcripts from the interviews and meetings was analysed (in part or in full) in four stages, referring to different levels. The first stage was a computer-assisted corpus linguistic analysis, using software which detects recurrent uses of 'keywords' (see Yates, 2001, pp. 93–146, for a detailed example). This is close to the ideal of an objective or technical analysis, in that it is statistical; however, there will inevitably also be judgement and interpretation involved, in this case, in the research-ers' initial selection of a subset of meetings which they thought were most relevant to the company's strategy. They then conducted the keyword analysis on the transcripts from these selected meetings.

In contrast, in the second stage of the analysis, the researchers conducted an interpretive analysis of agenda items and related topics of discussion, looking for patterns of the discussion (including 'topic elaboration' and 'argumentation patterns') in order to identify the 'macro-topics', 'primary' and 'secondary' topics. The third stage of the analysis was to classify the various strategies of the leaders of the meetings, and the fourth to consider how these strategies were used to 'achieve consensus'. The multi-level analysis can therefore be described as moving, broadly, from what was discussed (topics) to how it was talked about, then to how the leaders intervened in the discussions and produced agreement.

The researchers identified five 'discursive leadership strategies' which were linked back to the two styles of leadership identified by previous writers (transactional and transformational). Following the multiple foci of CDA, these strategies are discussed in terms of various features, including the grammar and also the communicative functions (linguistic-pragmatic) of the talk. Although some of these features might seem sufficiently specific to be identified unquestionably, the analysis is not as objective or technical as, say, counting key words. The analysis is interpretive. The researchers conduct it as informed observers, able to understand the talk in context because of the knowledge they have built up through the ethnographic study, including their reading of 'confidential company documents'.

The five strategies identified by the researchers are as follows:

(1) *Bonding.* This is defined as 'the discursive construction of group identity that supports motivation to reach consensus and a decision' (p. 603). The authors suggest it is evidenced in a leader's use of the personal pronouns. Part of the analysis was to count the relative uses of individual ('I') and group ('we') references by the talk of someone chairing a meeting.

(2) *Encouraging.* This is a strategy to open up general discussion and encourage other speakers to participate in order to promote a sense of the decisions being made by the group as a whole. The features of the talk which are taken as evidence of this include linguistic-pragmatic features such as questions to invite others to express their opinions, and 'the questioning/supporting of existing propositions, via repetition, positive back-channeling and explicit praise' (p. 604).

(3) *Directing.* In contrast to the previous strategy, this involves closing down or resolving the discussion and is evidenced, unsurprisingly, by opposite features: making firm statements rather than asking open questions; summarising ('So . . .'), and privileging of the chair's views over those of others, including by 'blocking' what they say. Although it might seem possible to detect features like this by looking for specified details (statements, not questions; particular words), identifying the strategy also requires interpretation. For instance, the researchers cite examples of someone pointing to an architectural drawing and saying, 'Look at this building', which closes down the previous discussion, or making a joke, which has the same effect.

(4) *Modulating.* This strategy involves contextualizing an issue in terms of urgency by linking it to larger imperatives or threats, for example, by suggesting (or denying) that there is only a limited time in which to achieve something. Again, it is difficult to reduce this strategy to features or categories which can be identified without interpretation. The analyst will have to look at the functions of a particular utterance in context.

(5) *Re/Committing*. This is the strategy of moving from a shared understanding to an agreement to act. It often involves a reference to the future, so grammatically, a change of tense. It may also involve reference to people's duties or responsibilities, or an appeal to their values.

The researchers then discuss extracts from transcripts of meetings to show how the chair of the meetings uses the different strategies and how their use constitutes a leadership style. On the basis of the analysis, the researchers argue that 'an egalitarian leadership style positively influences the formation of consensus within a team and, importantly, increases the likelihood of a durable consensus being achieved' (p. 612).

It is important to note that the same leader can adopt different styles in different contexts, and the same strategies can to some extent be employed as part of different styles. For example, directing can close down discussion, as part of a more authoritarian style (corresponding to transactional leadership) but it can also be part of summarizing and therefore a step towards reaching consensus in a more egalitarian (transformational) style. As with other forms of discourse analysis, a constant or predictable connection is not assumed between a 'type' of person and a form of discourse or discursive practice.

More unusually, at some points in the analysis, the researchers speculate about the mental states of the speakers, suggesting, for example, that a chair has previously made a decision which he does not disclose during the meeting. This contrasts with approaches, such as conversation analysis, which avoid attributing intention to speakers (see the discussion on discourse analysis and psychology in Chapter 2). In this study, there is some implication that leadership strategies and styles are employed intentionally, at least to some degree. This would suggest that the research findings have practical implications: people can be taught to be more effective leaders. However, this is not stated directly.

### Learning from this example

The article by Ruth Wodak, Winston Kwon and Ian Clarke presents an example of the following:

- a discourse analytic study of leadership in organizations;
- a project which combines Critical Discourse Analysis and ethnography;

- an analysis of meeting talk;
- a study which combines analyses on different levels, linking a macro issue, the exercise of power through leadership, to language practices, including the use of argument and rhetoric, and the details of the language itself, including linguistic features;
- a relatively large-scale study involving more than one researcher;
- an analysis which is not confined to speakers' talk but also speculates about their intentions and other mental states.

## Concluding comments

The four articles which have been discussed in this chapter present some of the possibilities and varieties of discourse analytic research. All four articles are interdisciplinary, investigating issues and situations which are of interest to academics in several areas of the social sciences. However, the analytic approaches employed by Jovan Byford and Elizabeth Stokoe are more closely associated with discursive psychology (Stokoe's article was published in a psychology journal), including in the sources they cite.

As already noted, the researchers and authors describe their studies in different ways and employ different concepts. Kirsten Bell uses the term 'discourse' to refer to a family of words and images associated with a particular topic. Her discussion of 'lifestyle discourses' and 'health promotion discourses' includes reference to a 'nutritional discourse' which distinguishes between 'good' and 'bad' food. The discourse therefore links specific words (such as 'diet' or 'healthy eating') to values (here, 'good' and 'bad' categorizations for particular foods and eating habits) which in turn are connected to larger ideas (what you eat affects your health; you have a responsibility to monitor your eating; eating well can prevent the onset or recurrence of cancer) and consequently to activities and aspects of society which are not so easily contained in language (cancer support groups; nutrition as a field of professional training and qualification; the distinction between medical and other forms of treatment; the pressure which cancer patients may feel to monitor their behaviour and even take responsibility for having brought the disease on themselves).

Jovan Byford mostly uses the term 'discourse' to refer to the talk or language of a particular speaker or source. He refers to 'public discourse', for talk and publications which are directed to a wide public audience, and 'ecclesiastical discourse', for talk which is by and about religious matters, in contrast, say, to official political communications. He also refers to 'the discourse of the Right', meaning both the language *of* certain speakers, from a particular political position, and the words, images and meanings which make up or constitute their politics. Elizabeth Stokoe is interested in the discourses that 'shape our gendered world' and in how 'taken-for-granted "facts" about women's appropriate behaviour and characters are perpetuated in discourse', that is, in people's talk. For Wodak et al., the analysis of discourse involves multiple levels, from 'strategy' to the details of wording.

Published accounts of research findings from particular projects, like these four articles, do not usually include detailed descriptions of how the analyst worked with her or his data. Nonetheless, there are some points which can be noted.

The first is that all four projects were conducted by the academics who wrote up the research, sometimes with the involvement of others. Discourse analysis is often the work of a single academic who works through a data set, becoming familiar with it, exploring and making connections and building an interpretation and argument which is relevant to the starting concerns of the project. This may place a practical limit on the scale of a discourse analytic project, especially the quantity of data which can be worked with. However, joint analysis is possible, although usually only in a small team. (An example of how this might be done is presented in Chapter 4.) Bell's project involved a second researcher, although there is no indication that the analysis was a joint process. Kwon and Clarke conducted the data collection for their relatively large project, and then worked together with Wodak on the analysis.

A second point to note is that all the analyses were conducted across the data sets. In other words, they were not confined to discrete items like a single speech or document or even a single interviewee. Discourse analysis is concerned with language use as a social phenomenon and therefore necessarily goes beyond *one* speaker or *one* newspaper article to find features which have a more generalized relevance. This is a potentially confusing point because the publication of research findings is generally presented through examples and the analyst may choose a single example or case to *exemplify* the features to be discussed, but those features are only of interest as a social, not individual, phenomenon. Occasionally the particular case may be chosen precisely because it has a wider social importance, as with Byford's discussion of Bishop Velimirović as a focal figure in contemporary Serbian politics.

In all four studies, the researchers also worked with far more data than can ever be written up or published. Wodak et al. did include extended transcripts in appendices to their article, but these were still only a small part of their full data set. This links to a further point to note: as part of the familiarization process, the researchers in all four studies had collected background material. Such material is sometimes separate to the data which are analysed and sometimes has a different function in the study. For example, Bell's attendance at the support group sessions, recorded in her field notes, presumably provided some of details which assisted her analysis (background on her participants and their experiences; practical information about different treatments and their side effects, etc.). Her description of her research as 'ethnographic' marks this backgrounding as part of the research process. Some of her observations are included in her field notes. Byford had clearly researched Serbian history and collected other information as part of his extensive data set, all of which was necessary background to his analysis (e.g., the biography of Bishop Velimirović and the history of the treatment of Jewish people in Serbia and former Yugoslavia). Stokoe's analysis of Membership Categorization Devices draws on her own cultural knowledge, for example, about the meanings and associations attached to motherhood. She had also clearly learned about neighbourhood mediation services and the kinds of problems they commonly deal with, and had probably watched far more broadcast material than she eventually included in her data set. The analysis by Wodak et al. refers to details of the company's situation and the relationships between staff which the researchers had learned during their fieldwork. As these examples indicate, a discourse analytic project often involves the kind of background or support familiarization which will enable the researcher to conduct an analysis as an insider (or partial insider), and this may sometimes blur with the data collection.

The fourth and final point to note here is that the four analyses refer back to, and build on, the findings of previous research, and the concepts used. Like other research, discourse analysis is always located within a tradition of ongoing research, substantively, that is, in terms of the topic or problem being investigated, and methodologically, in terms of the particular approach and concepts which are employed. Two of the studies refer to named approaches, Membership Categorization Analysis and Critical

Discourse Analysis, but both developed these approaches to accommodate the requirements of the specific studies. The process of conducting a discourse analytic study is discussed in general terms in the next chapter.

## Summary

Chapter 3 has discussed four published studies as examples of discourse analytic research.

# 4 The usefulness of discourse analysis for social science researchers

The previous chapters have introduced theories and issues associated with discourse analysis, and discussed examples of published discourse analytic research. This chapter is the first of two which offer more practical guidance for researchers planning their own projects. It begins with a discussion of some of the reasons why researchers use discourse analysis. It then describes some of the different kinds of discourse data. The final section discusses briefly how to obtain data although, given the focus of the book on analysis, this cannot be a full guide to conducting empirical research. The section includes advice on collecting new data, selecting already existing or 'found' material as data and producing transcripts.

## Reasons to use discourse analysis

This section discusses four possible reasons to adopt a discourse analytic approach in a research project, and then two more which have been labelled 'half-reasons' because there is often confusion about their relevance for discourse analysis.

### Reason 1: To work with interesting data

Many aspects of research are enjoyable. Researchers become closely involved in the problems which they investigate. They work with theories which present them with new insights and questions. They have the satisfaction of producing findings which contribute to the further development of those theories, add to general understandings of the social world and also have direct practical applications. Discourse analytic research is also notable for the intrinsic interest of the material which researchers work with. As previous chapters have indicated, this can include conversations and interviews, observations of what people do and texts which have been produced for a wide range of purposes.

### Reason 2: To investigate the practices and interactions of ordinary social life

The research projects outlined in Chapter 3 show how language data can be analysed in investigations of ordinary talk: between disputing neighbours or people attending a support group or colleagues in a work meeting, and by politicians using language in ways which are familiar from newspapers, media interviews and party political broadcasts. Discourse analysis enables researchers to explore these everyday situations and practices as part of larger processes and social phenomena, such as a contemporary political project to construct a new nation; the racism which potentially excludes certain people from the nation; the leadership practices which facilitate the running of a large business organization; the social norms linked to gender identities which function to exclude and stigmatize certain people in more local contexts and interactions; and a society's beliefs about health and illness which may function to encourage lifestyles, for example, in relation to exercise and diet, but also to blame people for becoming ill. The main argument for approaching talk and language data as evidence of the practices and interactions of ordinary life comes from ethnomethodology, discussed in Chapter 2.

### Reason 3: To investigate a particular culture

Investigations of culture through texts of different kinds (images as well as writing) often draw on discourse analytic approaches, although they may not always be described as such. As Chapter 2 discussed, any study of culture raises issues of definition. Because this book is primarily concerned with social research, it is less focussed on art, music and literature, sometimes described as 'high culture', than culture in the more anthropological sense of lifestyle and shared customs and beliefs. The problem then becomes the limits of the culture which is being referred to. Are the research findings applicable to a national population as if that were bounded and uniform? A further problem here can be that different languages can be assumed to relate to distinct cultures, which logically is not the case (Bell's study, discussed in Chapter 3, collected data from two language groups *within* the same nation-state, Canada). In short, the boundaries of any so-called cultural group are inevitably porous. The researcher must therefore decide whether any claims from the research have a broad reference, for example, Western culture, or a narrower one such as one age group in one country, or one kind of organization.

Most discursive researchers would probably make claims about a more local and specific cultural environment but they would also understand culture as complex and divided. An example of this position comes from Nigel Edley and Margaret Wetherell (1995) in their research on masculinity. They said: 'The cultural environment in which people live is not coherent and integrated ... but embodies a whole range of differences and contradictions.' Following Antonio Gramsci, the Italian Marxist, they suggest that 'society's common sense' is 'a fragmented body of ideas and practices, littered with the "sediments" or "deposits" of age-old ideas and theories' and 'an established stock of taken-for-granted understandings (which) can always provide the raw materials for the construction of markedly different world views' (p. 165). In the terms presented in this book, this common sense can be analysed in terms of discourses or discursive resources. The Membership Categorization Analysis which Elizabeth Stokoe employs (see Chapter 3) similarly refers to categories and connections which are taken for granted and can be understood to be part of common sense.

Common sense can therefore be understood as the shared possession of a whole society but it does not provide a single coherent cultural viewpoint for everyone in that society; its fragmented and mixed up character (with sediments from the past) can provide a basis for different and even conflicting arguments and perspectives. Discourse analysis informs the investigation of that kind of complexity, including its contradictions and conflicts, rather than any generalized claim about a society or cultural group. Analysts may investigate the conflicts and associated contests around power through an analysis in terms of 'ideology', as in the study by Jovan Byford. A key source for this approach is the work of Michael Billig (1996; 1999).

### Reason 4: To research identity

Researchers may employ discourse analysis to investigate 'big' categories of identity, such as national or gender identities, or they may begin with a narrower focus, such as illness or neighbour disputes or creative work, and then find in the course of the analytic process that identity becomes relevant. Some theoretical issues around identity were discussed in Chapter 2. Discourse analytic research on identities may focus on identities in context, as they are variously claimed, conferred, rejected and modified in ongoing talk, for example, between school pupils (Edley and Wetherell, 1997) or between people in a counselling situation (Edwards, 1998).

Another approach is to consider the identities associated with a particular life situation or problem, as evidenced in language data from many different people in that situation, such as cancer patients and their partners (Seymour-Smith et al., 2002; Bell, 2010), or people who live in one country but claim the national identity associated with another (Scully, 2009; 2010), or people at a similar point in their lives (Reynolds, 2006; 2008; McAvoy, 2009). The second approach may be linked to a theorization of identity or subjectivity which would not be described wholly or exclusively as discursive. Psychosocial research is broad-ranging but in some versions brings together an analysis of discourses and an interpretation using concepts associated with psychoanalysis (Hollway and Jefferson, 2000). Narrative-discursive research considers the resources and contingent constructions of sequence and consequence in people's talk, including their constructions of biographical narrative (Taylor and Littleton, 2006; Taylor, 2010).

### Half-reason 1: To obtain practical information about people's lives and experiences

This is probably the commonest purpose for which researchers collect language data, including talk, but it is labelled here as a 'half-reason' because it is not a priority for most discourse analysts.

Research for information tends to assume that language is referential or transparent; it is a channel or medium for carrying information from one person to another. Journalists make this assumption when they interview eye witnesses or experts, asking them to describe or explain something that has happened. However, most discourse researchers start from a different premise; they are interested in talk or language use as functional and constitutive.

The distinction can be confusing for two reasons. The first is that the same data can be employed for studies with both purposes; the difference is in the analysis, not the data collection. (The same language data can of course be repeatedly analysed in different ways: see Van Den Berg et al., 2003) The second is that although it is usual to make this distinction, between language as transparent and language as functional or constitutive, in practice the approaches are difficult to separate entirely. Using an interpretive or constructionist approach like discourse analysis does not exclude the use of talk as information. Moreover, even the writers who argue that language is constitutive also use language referentially in their own work, for example, when they describe what they did and present arguments and findings. An analysis will normally treat participants' accounts at least partly as information and in most research it is possible to accept these accounts as broadly truthful and reliable. As Martyn Hammersley has argued: 'No knowledge is certain, but knowledge claims can be judged in terms of their likely truth' (1998, p. 66).

### Half-reason 2: To explore people's opinions

Social psychologists, and especially those who employ discourse analytic approaches, have criticized the kinds of research which employ language data in order to investigate attitudes and opinions. They reject research which treats people's talk (or writing) as evidence of what they will say or do in future. They point out, for example, that an expression of prejudice is not necessarily proof that in some future situation the speaker will act in a prejudiced way (see Potter and Wetherell, 1987). In particular, discourse analysts criticize any assumption that a stated opinion is the straightforward expression of an attitude, as if this were some fixed mental state. They therefore avoid research which employs questionnaires or interviews with the purpose of collecting opinions or measuring or evaluating attitudes.

This rejection of conventional opinion polls and attitude research follows from two arguments associated with discourse analysis. The first is the argument that language is not transparent, as discussed above. What someone says will be shaped by the immediate context, including by what has come before. It is not direct evidence of the workings of the person's thoughts or mind. This links to the second argument, concerning the nature of the person. As discussed in Chapter 2, discourse analysts and discursive psychologists would reject the whole model of the person as a kind of container for inner states or processes.

What are the practical consequences for discourse analytic research? Discourse analytic research may investigate the ideas and ways of talking which function to exclude certain groups of people in society (Wetherell and Potter, 1992). This is likely to involve an exploration of discursive resources. They may consider the functions of (apparently) prejudiced talk in a specific context (Condor, 2011). Jovan Byford's research, discussed in Chapter 3, illustrates both these points. In summary, discourse analysis explores ideas which are commonly held across society or particular social groups or contexts, but they generally do not investigate or make claims about the opinions of individuals.

## Different forms of data

Discourse analysts work with many different kinds of language material. The research projects discussed in Chapter 3 illustrated the most common types. Kirsten Bell interviewed participants and also compiled field notes in her role as a participant-observer in cancer support groups. Jovan Byford conducted interviews, which he recorded, and also collected a range of texts which were publicly available, for example, in newspapers. Elizabeth Stokoe arranged for mediation sessions to be recorded and also collected recordings of television interviews. Wodak et al. recorded meetings and other events taking place within a business organization. Discourse studies can also analyse data which are not linguistic. For example, a study of nations and national identity might consider the ways in which flags are displayed (Billig, 1995), research on gender might discuss still or filmed images in advertisements (e.g., Gill, 2008).

Discourse analysts work with written language, for example, in the form of official documents, news articles and online material from web pages and forums. They analyse audio and video recordings. Although some researchers do work directly with the recordings, listening and watching repeatedly, the recordings are usually converted to written form through selective copying of what is said. This process of transcription is discussed below.

In summary, we can distinguish two categories of data. The first is new material which is collected specifically for a research project, such as interview and focus group recordings, and the second is already existing material (TV and radio programmes, newspapers, etc.). A researcher who collects *new* material may need to recruit potential participants, with all the steps this involves, including appropriate ethical procedures. The discourse analyst will not always be the interviewer or focus group leader. For example, Bell's data included recordings from a focus group conducted by someone else and Taylor and Littleton's research on creative work and creative careers (Taylor and Littleton, 2008) used interviews conducted by someone else, employed because she had particular interviewing skills. A possible intermediate category of material is the recording of talk and interactions which would have taken place anyway, whether or not the researcher was involved. Examples of this were Stokoe's mediation sessions and Wodak et al.'s meetings. This kind of data is often referred to as 'naturally occurring'. It is favoured by researchers working in the tradition of conversation analysis but is also used by other discourse researchers, as in Wodak et al.'s CDA study.

The material which discourse researchers work with does not automatically acquire the status of data. It needs to be collected and selected and often transformed in other ways. The next section discusses some of the processes involved. It provides practical guidance on obtaining data for discourse analysis. However, note that this is not a general guide to setting up and conducting an empirical project so it does not include advice on project design, obtaining access and contacting participants, implementing appropriate ethical procedures and other necessary aspects of any research project.

## Obtaining data

This section will discuss the practical side of discourse research, specifically issues of data collection and data processing, including transcription and selection.

Planning any research project, whatever the data to be used, involves establishing a theoretical and empirical starting point. This is given partly by key theoretical sources and previous empirical research. Both of these will shape the particular problem or research questions which a new project addresses. The researcher will need to decide what a data analysis might contribute, what specific analytic approach to use and what data are appropriate to it. (As just one example, a conversation analyst would probably not use interview data.) These decisions will help the researcher either to devise an appropriate method of data collection, such as setting up interviews or focus groups, arranging to record naturally occurring talk, observing and recording in a situation in which the researcher is also a participant, or to select the already existing data which are relevant to the project.

The studies discussed in Chapter 3 referred to data which had been obtained in several different ways: 'found' data (the different kinds of news material analysed by Byford, and the television interviews analysed by

Stokoe), new data obtained through interviews (by Byford, Bell and Wodak et al.), 'naturally occurring' data (the recorded mediation sessions analysed by Stokoe and the meetings analysed by Wodak et al.), and observation data obtained through participation (by Bell and her co-researcher, and by Kwon and Clarke, recorded in field notes). The last mentioned form of data is associated with ethnographic research. This is a research approach in its own right so it will not be covered here. The remainder of this section will address three questions: 'How do I select "found" data?' 'How do I collect data through interviewing?' and 'How do I obtain naturally occurring data?' The section leads into the discussion of the process of analysis in the next chapter.

### How do I select 'found' data?

A researcher who decides to analyse already existing material might appear to have an easier task than one who collects new data. However, there will still be a number of steps to follow before available material can be approached as research data. A major problem with found data is usually to narrow down the available material to a manageable quantity. Newspapers (now mostly available online), web forums, advertisements and official documents are all potentially excellent research material, as are existing sound and visual recordings from the web (again), television and radio but the researcher will almost certainly obtain more material than can be analysed. The problem will be to make a manageable and appropriate selection.

A further issue is to decide what material potentially constitutes data and what provides background information: as the studies in Chapter 3 illustrated, the distinction may not be clear. In general, the data for a discourse analytic study will be explored in terms of one of the analytic concepts associated with the approach, such as strategies, discourses, subject positions, dilemmas and Membership Categorizations.

### How do I obtain naturally occurring data?

As already noted, 'naturally occurring' usually refers to talk which would have happened anyway, whether or not the researcher had been there. One way to obtain this is to analyse talk which has already been recorded for another purpose, which is a form of found data. An example would be when the researcher chooses to analyse television or radio programmes, or online material. The practical advantages of using already recorded material are obvious; the disadvantages are that there may not be sufficient information available about the context (e.g., when the recording took place). The material may have been edited. There may also be some ethical issues involved about who has the rights to the material and, in some cases, whether it is appropriate to discuss speakers who cannot remain anonymous, for instance, because they were recorded for television or radio and named in the programme.

Alternatively, the researcher may arrange to obtain new data of this kind; for example, Wiggins (2004) invited families to record their meal-time conversation and many other researchers have placed recording equipment in schools and universities (of course with permission). Some of the most famous conversation analytic research has used recorded telephone calls (e.g., in the work of Harvey Sacks; see Jefferson, 1992). A study which seeks to obtain new data of this kind will of course involve the same steps (planning, obtaining ethical approval, calling for volunteers, etc.) as other research projects involving participants. These steps are not detailed in this book since it focuses primarily on analysis.

## How do I collect data through interviewing?

The most popular way to obtain data for discourse analysis is probably through interviewing. There are many published texts on research interviewing and this section will not attempt to provide a general guide but will focus on points relevant to interviewing for a discourse analytic project.

The first point to note is that the data which will be used are the talk, not the speakers. It is always tempting to attempt to 'understand' the person behind the talk but this is not the aim of most discourse analyses. The purpose of the interview is therefore an occasion for the collection of talk data. Because an interview is a form of interaction, a further purpose will be for the interviewer (who may not be the same person as the researcher) to engage in an interaction with the interviewee. There are many different types of interviews, from television interrogations of politicians to job recruitment interviews to consultations between medical doctors or therapists and their patients. A research interview is different from any of these but can occasionally take on aspects of all of them, especially if the researcher has not thought through the purpose and nature of the interview as an occasion. Most discourse analysts will aim for an interview which is something like a friendly conversation, that is, courteous, informal and two-way, with the interviewer acknowledging what is said, contributing responses and perhaps some thoughts and experiences of her own.

The interaction between researcher and participant begins well before the interview. Because discourse theories emphasize the situated nature of talk, it will be relevant for the researcher to pay careful attention to the way the project is presented to potential participants and the expectations which may be established, for example, in how the interview is set up and what they are invited to talk about. Most research participants volunteer or agree to be interviewed because they have some interest in the general topic of the research. However, they may also have misunderstood the topic, however carefully they have been briefed, and even the purpose of the interview, making assumptions, for example, about the kind of information or details which are required.

The researcher has a responsibility towards the participants. Ideally they will enjoy the interview: it is a situation in which they are receiving attention and interest. Occasionally they may be involved because they disagree with the researcher's position, so that the interview is a form of contest (this might have been the case with Byford's interviews, referred to in Chapter 3). In either case, the researcher is the beneficiary, receiving vital contributions to her or his research project, and the interviewee deserves to be treated with courtesy and, if at all possible, not caused distress or offence.

Many discourse researchers prefer to conduct their own interviews but others work from the recordings and transcripts of interviews conducted by someone else. The research data will include both the answers provided by the participant and the questions and other contributions from the interviewer since these are all part of the interaction. The most common type of interview is a semi-structured interview, that is, one in which the interviewer has a prepared list of questions which is used as a general guide but not a rigid template for the interview. For instance, the interviewer may omit or rephrase questions or vary the order, depending on what has already been said.

An important premise in discourse analytic research is that the talk is prompted by the questions but not produced by them. The talk is co-constructed in the interaction: this is part of its situated nature. It is also shaped by the discursive resources which are available to speakers. In addition, depending on the topic of the interview, much of the talk is likely to be rehearsed, produced on this occasion as a situated version of what has been said before. These various assumptions suggest different approaches to analysis (discussed in the next chapter) and also have implications for the researcher planning an interview. There is an argument that an interview cannot 'fail' because any talk, or even an absence of response, can constitute data and be analysed (see Jones, 2003, for an analysis of an interview which went wrong). However, for novice researchers in particular, it will be preferable to have more talk rather than less, so ideally the interview questions will be easy for the participant to understand; they will be open-ended and interesting, inviting extended answers, and they will encourage a flow from one topic or area to the next without any abrupt change of focus to interrupt the interview as a conversation.

The researcher will of course need to decide how many interviews to conduct. Since the aim is to analyse talk data, not participants, a discourse analytic study seldom involves just one or two interviews. A fairly substantial data set or body of interview material is appropriate. For a researcher working alone, 15 to 20 interviews are probably the minimum. These might be obtained from 20 participants, or 10 who are interviewed twice. Repeat interviews, associated with a longitudinal study, can enable interesting comparisons across different occasions of talk (see Taylor, 2012), as can data from different sources, such as group discussions and one-to-one interviews.

Regardless of the number of interviews conducted, they will almost certainly be recorded for later transcription and analysis. Most researchers in this field use audio recordings but video can provide useful additional information, for example, about exactly who is speaking in a group interview or focus group.

### Producing transcripts

In its simplest form, transcription is the process of converting talk to written language by writing down what was said. It is part of the analytic process (Ochs 1979; Hammersley, 2010) but it is only the beginning. As the next chapter discusses, the process of analysing interview transcripts requires protracted and iterative re-reading and comparison, across different interviews and different parts of the same interview. The initial purpose is to find patterns in the data and this provides a useful, general guide for transcription. The details to be transcribed will be those in which the analyst seeks to find patterns. For example, if the interest is in discursive resources, such as discourses, interpretative repertoires or narratives, then the most important content of the transcript will be the words. If the analyst is studying interaction, for example, in a conversation analytic study, then the transcript will need to record details of the interaction, such as the pauses or overlaps between successive turns of talk from different speakers. Researchers have devised systems of 'notation' for recording various details (hesitation, intonation, emphasis) and particular studies may devise new symbols to indicate particular points of interest. Chapter 3 showed an example of a detailed transcript from the article by Stokoe.

Transcription is not a purely technical process because it is always selective: it involves interpretation. There is almost no limit to the details which can potentially be included, depending on the researcher's interest, so it is never possible to transcribe 'everything'. Some analysts do all of their own transcription, regarding this as a necessary part of the process of familiarizing themselves with their data. Others employ a professional transcriber to produce a first version and in the near future, this may be done using voice recognition software. However, the analyst generally needs to check such transcripts against the original recordings and correct and add details. Some researchers begin by working with recordings and part-transcripts, then produce final transcripts of selected sections of the data rather than attempting to transcribe the entire data set. Whatever choice is made, transcription is a laborious and time-consuming task.

There are three further points to be made about transcripts. The first is that a transcript is primarily a working document for the researcher. Research publications such as reports, articles and monographs will include transcript extracts but, as with other data, the discourse researcher will always have analysed more material than can be presented to readers. A transcript can seldom be published in full, partly for this reason of length, partly because there will too much detail which is irrelevant to the arguments of the researcher and partly because there will be details which breach anonymity. (For example, a single reference to a detail like a participant's occupation or age or place of residence will probably not enable others to identify her, but if at various points in her talk she discloses several of those details, then taken together they may enable other people to recognize her or find out who she is.) This therefore becomes an ethical problem, since participants are usually promised anonymity.

The second point is that even the simplest transcription of talk will be different from written language because the grammar of talk is different from the grammar of writing. This is a linguistic point which does not need to be explored here, except to point out that people do not speak in 'correct' sentences. Newspapers sometimes present interviews as if these have been directly transcribed, but the talk has generally been quite extensively edited into the form of standard written language, in full sentences (indicated with capital letters, full stops and commas). Unedited talk always contains repetitions, incomplete utterances, false starts, hesitations and self-corrections, so transcribed talk generally includes at least some of these regularities. A 'found' transcript may provide suitable material for analysis, but the analyst will need to be aware of how it has been edited and what may have been omitted, or added.

A third point which sometimes concerns researchers is whether or not they should ask participants to check the transcripts of interviews. It is usual to offer people a transcript of their own interview but it is important to be clear why this is done. First, it is a courtesy. Second, it may also be done for ethical reasons, for example, to offer participants an opportunity to ask for certain details to be removed, although that is not usually necessary if participants have been promised anonymity. A third reason, in a longitudinal study, is that a participant may be given a transcript as preparation for a subsequent interview, to remind them of what was said. An argument against this is that remembering is selective (i.e., it always involves forgetting) so that participants may be surprised and even distressed to read in a transcript what they said on a previous occasion, especially some time ago. A different reason for not returning a transcript is that people are often disconcerted by the irregularity of transcribed talk because they are not aware that this is different from written language, as noted above. More prosaically, transcripts are very long so the participant is being given quite a substantial reading task. If a reminder is really needed, then it is probably more appropriate for the researcher to prepare a short summary of key points covered in the previous interview.

Some researchers, such as oral historians, do give back transcripts as part of a process of negotiating a factual record. The participant is encouraged to revise what was said. However, a discourse analyst is interested in the situated nature of talk and would not expect people to give identical accounts in different interviews. If a participant amends a transcript (e.g., by adding details) what results will be a composite of several versions from different occasions. Such a composite is not a transcript in discourse analytic terms so is not appropriate as data for the kind of analyses discussed in this book.

## Summary

Chapter 4 has discussed some reasons to use discourse analysis for a research project, the kinds of data which can be analysed and the commonest ways of obtaining data.

# 5 The challenges of discourse analysis

This chapter reviews the problems or challenges faced by the discourse analyst. The content of this chapter also complements the section 'Obtaining data', in Chapter 4, as a practical guide, moving on from the task of obtaining data to the process of analysis and interpretation. The chapter is organized in a question and answer format.

## How do I decide the right approach to discourse analysis for my project?

As the previous chapters of this book have indicated, there is no one 'right way' to analyse discourse. Any discourse analytic project establishes its own connections between the researcher's assumptions about the world (theory), the topic being investigated, the interpretation of 'discourse' which is adopted, the materials to be analysed (data) and the relevance of those materials to the topic (such as when talk is analysed as 'identity work'). A new project may build on previous research or it may develop its own unique variant; the resulting project may or may not be labelled discourse analysis. As a consequence, the researcher needs to be aware of the assumptions underlying the methods she or he employs. Most researchers will begin by reading published studies (like the ones in Chapter 3) alongside the work of key theorists (such as those named in Chapter 2). The reference lists for publications can indicate other relevant sources. The broad approach given by previous work can then be revised during the planning of the new project and new analytic concepts may be incorporated when the researcher begins working with the data, but at every stage it will be important to check decisions back against the underlying theory.

## How do I decide how much material to analyse?

This is a difficult point. It is certainly possible to have too small a quantity of data. The analytic process outlined in Chapter 5 involves searching for patterns across a data set, and this would not be possible with, say, just one interview or one document. Alternatively, with that amount, it would still be possible to build on the findings of previous research, to note that the new data illustrate patterns and features noted by other researchers. For example, a conversation analyst might label details of a new extract of talk with reference to the canon of conversation analytic studies. There is an assumption operating in this approach that interactions can be described in near-universal terms, but most other discourse researchers would not generalize so widely and so they work with larger data sets.

On the other hand, there are practical limits to the quantities of data which are manageable. For instance, recorded material probably needs to be transcribed, which is a laborious process, as noted in the previous chapter. More importantly, the researcher needs to familiarize herself with all or most of the data, as discussed in the following section.

It might seem obvious that collecting more data will raise the standard of the research and the reliability of the findings, but this is a misconception. First, qualitative research does not and cannot use statistically representative samples; the basis for generalization is different (see later). Second, the research process is not equivalent to drawing a very detailed picture, adding detail to achieve a closer representation of reality. Rather, the researcher is building a chain of argument, linking (i) a theory of how the social world works, and (ii) a second theory (usually called methodology) of how material collected in an empirical study can be treated as evidence of the workings of that world, to (iii) the selection and presentation of particular material (data) as the evidence to support a new claim. Adding more and more data does not inevitably strengthen the links; the more important point is how they are theorized.

## How do I manage and 'process' my data?

Most researchers work with a combination of electronic files, for easy storage, and hard copy printouts, for easy reading, re-reading and marking up. The software packages which are rather misleadingly referred to as CAQDAS (computer assisted qualitative data analysis software) cannot analyse discourse data, or any other qualitative data, because the researcher will always need to familiarize her or himself with all of the material and interpret it, a process which inevitably involves decision-making. However, software is extremely useful as another medium for marking up data like transcripts, and for appending comments and sorting material into new files, especially when there is more than one researcher working on the project.

## How do I begin the analysis?

The process of analysing discourse data is not linear but exploratory and iterative. In other words, the analyst's task is not one of straightforwardly 'translating' or 'decoding' the data, one item at a time; rather, analysis involves reading and re-reading an entire data set, comparing, noticing and marking points of possible interest and returning to them later. (The analysts whose work is discussed in Chapter 3 all worked 'across' their data sets, as noted in the section 'Concluding comments'.) This is a time-consuming process and most novices do not allow enough time for it. The analysis phase of a discourse analysis project may overlap with both the data collection and the writing up and will take longer than either. It cannot be accomplished in one or two sittings.

Without computers (and many analysts do prefer to work with hard copies of transcripts and other data), starting the analysis may involve marking selected sections of the data, perhaps with different coloured pens; assembling piles or files of 'like' material; scribbling notes and making lists of possible points for follow up, often working from features and concepts noted by previous researchers. Many analysts now use software to facilitate the same operations. A standard word-processing program can be used to copy and paste sections of data into new files and mark up points of interest. So-called qualitative analysis software facilitates all of these operations and is particularly useful for coordinating the work of a team of researchers. Some software, such as the corpus analysis programme used by Wodak et al., searches out particular word sets. However, as noted above, most software is designed as a tool for data *management* rather than analysis. The hard work of exploring, thinking and decision-making still has to be done by the analyst.

As the analyst becomes familiar with all of the data, one activity will be to mark connections between different pieces of material, even though in the first instance the significance of the connection may not be apparent, and then to assemble subsets or collections of material. This operation is often referred to as 'coding'. Initially, the codes may be very broad (e.g., 'work', 'home', 'finance') and they will not be exclusive: the same piece of material may be coded several ways. Coding cannot be done mechanically, without active thinking, although it is often possible use a computer search function in order to find potentially relevant material, for example, by looking up key words relevant to a code. Coding can be a useful 'way in' to a large data set but it is not the inevitable starting point.

For interview data, another starting point can be to compare different participants' answers to the same or similar questions. When the same participant has been interviewed more than once, there can be comparisons across the interviews. Since the talk is situated, it is not likely that someone will say exactly the same thing on different occasions, but both the difference and the similarities can be surprising. In a narrative-discursive analysis, one point of interest is the similarities which follow from the rehearsed nature of many accounts, so that previous versions, for example, of a speaker's life history, become resources for her own subsequent talk: Taylor and Littleton call these 'local resources' (2006, p. 33; 2012, p. 42).

More generally, similarities across interviews (whether in the actual wording, the images or broad ideas, or the style or form of talking) can usefully be grouped together for a later decision about how to relate the material to analytic concepts such as discursive resources. A different starting point will be to consider the talk as action: What is it doing in this specific interaction and more generally? It may be useful here to think about rhetorical work, of the kind discussed by Byford. This is talk or writing which makes an argument, sometimes by anticipating a challenge or criticism ('I'm not prejudiced but ...'), indicating the argumentative and dialogic nature of talk (Billig, 1987; 1999). The relevant analytic concepts will be given, at least initially, by the approach which the researcher has chosen (see question 1, 'How do I decide the right approach to discourse analysis for my project?'). As the analysis proceeds, new concepts may be taken up. For example, an investigation of how participants resist dominant discourses (as in Bell's study, discussed in Chapter 3) might focus attention on the uses of humour. The researcher would then return to the data looking for jokes, laughter and so on. New questions arise: Are there different kinds of laughter? What is the significance of speakers laughing together or one person laughing alone? This point would suggest new features to be included in the transcription, and so on.

The researcher's interpretation is based on evidence obtained through a rigorous data analysis, but this analysis remains hidden to a great extent. One reason is that the quantities of data involved cannot be presented, for practical reasons of length and also, of course, to protect the anonymity of participants. Discourse analysis is therefore an interpretative analytic approach grounded in the evidence provided, for example, from transcribed talk. The previous painstaking exploration of multiple interviews has to be taken on trust. (This is not very different to the 'off-stage' work involved in most kinds of qualitative research.)

A discourse analyst detects a pattern in the data and eventually labels it for the purposes of the particular discussion. Clearly, this is a loose process of labelling rather than a right/wrong identification. For example, what one researcher calls a narrative, that is, a construction of sequence and consequence, often with a link to temporality, could be a part of what another analyst would call an interpretative repertoire.

The remainder of this section presents two examples of the beginning of the analytic process, one of a researcher working alone and one of collaborative analysis between two researchers. Although many discourse analytic projects are conducted by a single researcher, there is a sense in which no academic researcher is working entirely alone because she or he is necessarily engaging with others by reading their work, listening to conference presentations and presenting papers to journals and conference audiences for feedback. Discourse analytic researchers are also likely to seek opportunities to present data or work in progress in seminars and research groups. Other people's suggestions can provide an invaluable stimulus for an analyst who is struggling with a large data set.

### Example 1

A researcher is analysing interview and observation data which she has collected in a project working with young people. Her first task is to re-read her field notes and interview transcripts and notes, at least twice over for each. She does this over several days in a number of sessions, some of them quite short (even as little as half an hour). As she reads, she tries to keep an open mind, putting aside, temporarily, her own views of her participants and their lives and her knowledge of other research and of theories. This is sometimes referred to as 'bracketing': the purpose is to approach the data *as* data without thinking too much about the speakers themselves or the situations or events which are referred to. A group discussion and brainstorming of a sample of data can help the researcher to do this; the views of other people draw her attention to her own assumptions.

She marks sections of the talk which seem interesting for any reason, such as wording which is striking, or a memorable anecdote or interaction. She also notes features which recurred within one speaker's talk (wording, references, accounts), possibly on different occasions, or across the talk of different speakers, or across several kinds of data (e.g., links between what one participant said and what the researcher had observed another participant do).

The researcher then goes back to the marked sections of the data and re-reads those. She re-examines sections of interview data on several levels, asking herself questions.

- The first is the level of the interview interaction between the interviewer and participant. She asks: What function does the talk have as a response to questions and follow-on to previous discussion? Her purpose here is to examine the talk as interaction between the people who were present. A further step is to consider whether there is interaction with other potential or imagined audiences. Are certain features of the talk addressed to people who are not present, such as potential critics? Her purpose here is to consider the rhetorical aspects of talk. For example, negative prefacing comments like 'I'm not saying that …' are generally seen to be directed, or oriented, in this way (cf. Byford's study in Chapter 3).
- The second level relates to the talk more generally. Possible questions to ask are: What features of the talk itself are noticeable? Are there stories or anecdotes which have a rehearsed feel, or are even repeated? What positive and negative valuing appears? What's mentioned as 'good' or 'bad' for example? Are there instances of implied cause and effect, that is, what's spoken of as leading to or following from something else? What categorization appears in the talk? The purpose here is to examine the talk as a complex changing production which is shaped both by previous talk and ideas (the speaker's own, and other people's) and by its multiple, overlapping functions as communication, with the interviewer and with other audiences associated with particular subject positions (imagined listeners, society in

general, etc.). This contributes to an analysis of the talk in terms of discursive resources.

- The third level is the most straightforward and the one common to other qualitative approaches, like ethnography, which treat the speaker as an informant. She asks: What's happening in the events described in the talk?

She compiles files of some of these features and labels the patterns for reference, but at this point she does not try to explain their importance.

### Example 2

Two researchers are analysing 50 interviews which have been conducted for a large project by a research fellow, then transcribed. The researchers have listened to each recording and read each transcript as they received them. They then begin the process of analysis.

- They choose an interview to study closely. Each listens again to the recording and re-reads the transcript, making their own notes.
- They meet. Each reports what she's noticed about the interview and one makes expanded notes which she writes up as a record.
- They repeat this process over different meetings, discussing two or three interviews at each meeting. They start to see similar points recurring in different interviews, or at different points in the same interview. The notes on each interview begin to reflect these patterns, which they label (e.g., 'big money talk', 'a story about childhood', 'competition').
- The researchers continue the process for all the interviews, which takes hours! By the time they have discussed about half their data, they have labelled a number of patterns and are talking about how these fit together, why they might be there (e.g., what functions they might fulfil) and what implications they might have. A useful point can be the examples which depart from a pattern (Taylor and Littleton, 2006, discuss an example of an analysis which builds on a pattern and exceptions). The researchers also consider how these patterns fit with points which other analysts have noted, and with theories. Some ideas and possible arguments begin to emerge in their discussion. The researchers note these but are careful not to close down the process of exploration. They also consider their own preconceptions, discussing what they might be wanting to find or,

alternatively, avoiding seeing. What personal interests are they bringing to the data? Which participants do they feel more or less interest in, and why? Are there any interviews they should read again, putting aside certain assumptions?

- They choose particular patterns which they have noted and return to individual interviews where the pattern appeared, looking again at the pattern within the context of the particular interview.

## How do I develop an interpretation and argument?

At this point, the researcher, whether working alone or with someone else, will be very familiar with a large proportion of the data, not just one or two interviews. She has picked out recurring features and compiled collections of examples of these features. The next step is less systematic. The researcher steps back from the data to the larger foci, which are the following:

- the research questions which were the starting point for the whole project,
- the issues given by the theoretical background to the project and by previous related research.

By relating the patterns to analytic concepts (discourses, categories, strategies), the researcher develops an account of what is happening in the talk. This leads on to the questions: What could this be evidence of? What do I want to argue on the basis of this evidence?

The point of a discourse analytic project using talk data is that the theory underpinning the project indicates a particular connection between the talk and the larger question or problem being addressed. The aim is not to analyse the speaker as a person. For researchers working with talk data, it will therefore be useful at this point to try to put aside what is known of the person and focus only on the talk. This is more easily done some time after the occasion of the interview, or with data from an interview conducted by someone else.

The aim now is to build up arguments, from evidence to claims. It will probably be useful to build on similarities and differences compared to the evidence and claims of previous researchers in this area. This thinking process is the most difficult part of analysis and interpretation. It will almost inevitably involve many drafts of notes and trial arguments. On the way, some arguments, even with evidence, will be put aside, while others will be rehearsed and refined.

The eventual core argument which will be presented in a research text (a paper or a chapter of a dissertation or thesis) will be the outcome of this extended process of development; the process itself and most of the data cannot be presented in full. Discourse researchers are always looking for succinct data extracts which *exemplify* patterns that recurred across an entire data set. Sometimes it is practical to discuss a single case in this way (e.g., Taylor, 2011) but the discussion will make clear how far this case is representative of the larger data set, including the ways in which it is distinctive. Talk or field notes can provide illustrative examples of general features but any example will inevitably be rich in specific details, some of which are particular to one participant or speaker. Part of the task of writing up the analysis will be to draw attention to the general argument and claims being made on the basis of the entire data analysis.

## What is the status of the findings?

The findings of a discourse analytic study are an interpretation grounded in a rigorous process of data analysis. Generalization is on the basis of the patterns found in a large body of talk or other language data through the analytic process described above. The broad assumption is that the analysis has discovered social meanings and language-related practices which are a feature of a wider context and population. However, there is no assumption that either the meanings or practices are wholly determining or predictive of future practices, interactions or situations. Social life is assumed to be emergent and highly complex. Consequently, although any example of talk is from an individual speaker, potentially describeable in general category terms (a woman or a man, of a certain age, occupation and so on), the speakers are not discussed or analysed as 'types'.

## Summary

Chapter 5 answered some common questions about the challenges of discourse analysis, including the process of analysis.

# 6 Criticisms of discourse analysis

This chapter will be presented in the form of 'critical statements' followed by discussion.

## 'Discourse analysis is just about words'

This criticism encompasses several different issues. A statement like this is usually part of a larger complaint that discourse analysis does not take account of something else, such as non-verbal communication, body language and emotions, visual representations, or objects, space and the material world, including people's bodies. A number of points can be made in response. In addition, the criticism can refer to how discourse analysts discuss their participants: this is explored as a separate statement in the section 'Discourse analysis doesn't take enough account of people'.

The first point to make here is to agree that, yes, for some discourse analysts the approach *is* about words and language. They investigate how texts and talk in certain contexts contribute to the exercise of power. Parliamentary speeches, news reports, official statements and other forms of public communication, such as advertisements, can all be analysed with this focus. The interest is in how language is used to reinforce norms, legitimate existing social structures, subtly obscure or rationalize inequalities, play down problems and perpetuate an interpretation of society which supports some interests and obscures others. Analysts aim to expose these effects and in doing so, to challenge established orders and elites. The analysis of the texts may extend beyond the words themselves to the visual elements of a text, such as the organization of a news page with headlines and pictures. However, the main focus will almost certainly be on the language. The approach known as Critical Discourse Analysis, associated with Norman Fairclough, Ruth Wodak and Teun A. van Dijk among many others, is particularly known for this kind of research.

A second reason why some (but not all) analysts would agree with the above statement is that words and language have a special status in society. When people talk to each other their language use may incorporate gestures (such as a nod of the head) and sounds which are not words ('Mm' or similar as an acknowledgement or agreement) but these are meaningful within a communication system which is primarily verbal. There are special cases in which an entire 'conversation' can be conducted without words, but they are rare exceptions. Communication through language use is a vital, rule-governed social practice in which people necessarily become skilled in order to function as members of society. Talk and language are therefore obvious forms of data for a social scientist who wants to study society. In an analysis of such data, a researcher can draw on her or his own expertise as a language user, as well as on previous findings about the conventions of conversation. The importance of this argument can be underlined by comparison with a research project in which the participants are asked to draw a picture or take a photograph. They are being asked to engage in an unfamiliar practice with few or no conventions. (Of course this may not be quite the case if they are skilled artists or photographers, and the analyst shares those skills, but that would be an exceptional situation and highly unusual in social research.) The consequence will be that neither the participants nor the analyst will be able to 'do' things with the media or interpret what is produced as either a communication or a socially meaningful activity. Alternatively, the researcher may invite them to talk about what they have produced, so that the analytic focus becomes, again, language.

However, some discourse analysts would disagree strongly with the statement that 'Discourse is *just* about words'. Their argument, broadly, is that there is no neat separation between the meanings in language and in the social world more generally. To talk about people, things and the material world is to bring them into language (and therefore 'into culture' in the words of Edwards et al., 1995). Even if people and things are not specifically named and described by a research participant, they inevitably function within larger systems of meaning. Previous chapters have discussed examples of the connections between certain named or nameable identities (a good learner, a healthy eater), the values and knowledge which makes the identities available, the institutions through which the knowledge is established and disseminated and so on. Some of this complex formation may operate without being explicitly brought into language: indeed, one purpose of the research may be to identify and name what has previously been invisible and unacknowledged. Words and language are inevitably linked with the social world and its ongoing activities. In this view, to say 'discourse analysis is just about words' is to ignore the social meanings which are attached to language and words yet not confined to them.

These issues arise partly because of the range of data and analytic approaches encompassed within the category 'discourse analysis'. Researchers who are interested in the difficult experiences of people who have been socially marginalized may feel that a focus on words and language amounts to a trivialization of their participants' difficulties. To study details of wording, grammar and punctuation may seem inappropriate, even offensive, and a turning away from vital, apparently non-verbal aspects of their participants' lives such as feelings, their poor health or physical injuries, bad living conditions or incarceration. A further motivation here may be a wish to look at the 'whole'. It may seem disrespectful to investigate only small details of an account.

One counter-argument is that the apparently non-verbal aspects of communication are generally connected to language, so language data can provide appropriate evidence. Another counter-argument is that all research involves the selective reduction of a complex social world to data. For example, a census or survey reduces people and their situations to categories and statistics, yet it can prompt help and improvement of their welfare. Discourse analytic research has always had a strong connection with social issues. As the previous chapters have indicated, discourse researchers have challenged prejudice, racism and other injustices. The analysis of words and language, often at the level of fine detail, is their starting point for doing this.

A final point to note here is the issue of emotions, more recently linked to the study of affect. Some psychosocial researchers have suggested that discourse analysis 'leaves out' emotion. The assumption here is that the taking up or contesting of a subject position is a verbal or intellectual action which is separate from feelings. This argument is possibly a consequence of an artificial separation of language data from the continuum of meanings, lived experience and so on with which it is implicated, as outlined earlier. A similar separation appears in the common contrasting of the rational with the emotional. A counter-argument would be that the types of discursive resources discussed by many analysts are laden with values and other affective associations so that the kind of identity work which may be investigated and discussed in terms of transcripts is, again, not just about words (see Taylor and Littleton, 2012).

## 'Discourse analysis doesn't take enough account of people'

Much of the discussion in this book has referred to the analysis of talk data from interviews and other interactions. For novice researchers in particular, there can be a tension between forms of data which appear to push attention towards the individual speaker, understood in commonsense terms as agentic and expressive, and an analytic approach which challenges this conception of the person (see Chapter 2) and makes claims about social phenomena rather than particular people. Researchers who collect their own data are likely to have a strong impression of speakers as driven by emotions and intentions, yet discourse analysis is concerned with meanings and practices which are primarily social, albeit impacting upon and constitutive of individuals and often investigated through their particular practices, including talk practices. (This is a reason to avoid giving participants pseudonyms or prefacing their discussions of data extracts with mini biographies of the speaker or writer: see Taylor, 2012.)

This tension is seldom directly addressed in published accounts of analyses or in research methods texts. Harvey Sacks, the originator of conversation analysis, famously said about people and their talk: 'Don't worry about how fast they're thinking.... don't worry about whether they're "thinking". Just try to come to terms with how it is that the thing comes off. Because you'll find that they can do these things' (Sacks in Jefferson, 1992, p. 11). This is another way of saying that the focus is on talk as a practice, a form of doing which (like body movements) is seldom pre-planned or consciously performed. As a consequence, analysts tend to avoid using language which implies a two-stage process of thinking and speaking. This is a subtle point, not least because, first, speaking can shift from a practice which is performed without intention to one which the speaker is very conscious of planning (e.g., in unfamiliar interactions), and second, because of course some analysts do investigate material which has been planned with great care and attention, such as political speeches on sensitive topics (as in Byford's research, discussed in Chapter 3).

Nonetheless, discourse analysis remains an approach primarily used for investigating collectively held meanings and collective practices. The additional issues of how these may be constitutive of the talk of an individual and, further, constitutive of the person as an individual are ones addressed by some social psychologists (e.g., Hollway and Jefferson, 2000; Wetherell, 2003; Taylor, 2011; 2010) but are not necessarily part of discourse analysis. This territory is one which is increasingly discussed as the concern of psychosocial research. For novice researchers, the important point to keep in mind is that discourse analysis is an approach for social research. It analyses language data but does not attempt to make claims about the characters and personalities of the people who produced the language, written or spoken. Discourse analysis is not about obtaining the kind of insights into individuals which are commonly associated with confession or therapy.

## 'Interviews are not an appropriate source of data'

Some discourse analysts oppose the use of interviews. They are mainly discursive psychologists who work in the tradition of conversation analysis (e.g., Potter and Hepburn, 2005). They argue that an interview is not a natural form of talk because the interviewer is imposing the topic on the participants and leading them to talk about things they wouldn't otherwise talk about. One counter-argument is that an interview is a familiar situation in which people 'naturally' produce a particular kind of talk, interview talk. A second, which rather contradicts the first, is that the talk in interviews is not completely different to talk in other contexts but will inevitably overlap in many respects, for example, in the ways in which speakers follow conventions or present new versions of previously rehearsed accounts (who I am, where I come from, where I work, a funny thing that happened to me, etc.).

A somewhat different defence of interviews is that the term 'naturally occurring' invokes a research paradigm which most discourse analysts would reject, that is, one associated with an objective researcher who discovers universal truths in a research situation which is 'uncontaminated' by the researcher's intervention or the expectations of the participants. This is generally referred to as positivism (see Hammersley and Atkinson, 2007). The contrasting position favoured by most social researchers is that no form of data collection is 'natural' or 'unnatural' and any data analysis, including discourse analysis, is inevitably interpretive, shaped to some extent by the researcher, even though she or he will attempt to be rigorous and systematic to limit personal bias. An analysis is always partial, and incomplete.

This alternative position draws attention to data collection and analysis as situated activities which occur within the context of the project, including its socio-historic and cultural context. This suggests that the researcher needs to take account of the expectations that participants may bring to an interview or any other form of participation in research, including to the 'naturally occurring' situations. It suggests too that both the data collection and the data analysis will have meanings particular to the time, place, participants, and so on. For example, the particular reference and associations of a word or image may go unrecognized if the researcher is not familiar with these larger contexts. A practical implication of this interpretive position is that the discourse researcher needs to collect additional material as part of the process of familiarizing her or himself with the context. This material will inform the analysis even though it will not be data. Chapter 3 noted the collection of such background material within the four studies discussed.

## 'Discourse analysis just produces interpretations, not facts'

This criticism relates to some of the points made above. It is linked to an assumption that facts and interpretations can be distinguished, and therefore to a notion of truth (see Chapter 2). Statistics, for example, seem to be uncontroversial because the counting can be checked. They are not, it seems, just one researcher's interpretation but an objective measure of the world as it is. However, a closer examination of the assumption will show the distinction to be unfounded. As just one point, what is counted must previously be defined, which involves interpretation and value judgements. A simple example, discussed by Raghuram (2009), is that official statistics on immigrants vary considerably depending on which people are deemed to be immigrants. The same will apply to other categorizations of people.

A further issue of particular concern for discourse analysts derives from the arguments of Schegloff (1997). His concern was that analysts would bring their own interests to talk data and freely interpret the talk as being 'about' that. Against an analyst who would look at a conversation between a man and a woman and decide that it is inevitably 'about' gender, Schegloff argued that a close analysis on CA principles could show whether or not gender was relevant, or salient, by revealing what the speakers themselves 'orient to' or 'make relevant'. This is also an argument against 'reading off' certain behaviours as gendered. If a man speaks at the same time as a woman, is this inevitably evidence of interruption and a performance of a gendered identity of dominance? Might it not be an example of overlapping talk as a common form of agreement in the talk of people who position themselves as equals?

Schegloff's arguments are a useful challenge to the over-free interpretation of data. Given that any two speakers can be categorized in terms of multiple differences (e.g., gender, age, sexuality, nationality, place of birth, occupation, religion, body features such as height, education), how reasonable is it to claim that their conversation is relevant evidence for a study of any particular category? On the other hand, there seems no reason to assume that people may not 'orient to' several different issues at once simultaneously, so that talk may be 'about' gender as well as its ostensible topic. Theorists of intersectionality (e.g., Phoenix and Pattynama, 2006) argue that categorization is always complex; for example, the relevant identification will be as a raced, classed, gendered person of a certain age group. Discourse research on prejudice and racism has shown how categories may merge, so that 'culture' becomes synonymous with 'race'. More subtly, the conventional categories of research may be overtaken by new lived categories of identity and difference, such as the 'postcodes' currently invoked in conflicts between some young people in London. A discourse analyst needs to be alert to all of these possibilities, to be alive to the possible differences between participants' views and her own, and to pause repeatedly to interrogate the assumptions and concerns she brings to the research.

These further issues can be followed up in the sources listed in the recommended reading list at the end of the book. The more general point to note is that yes, discourse analysis is interpretive *as is other research*, qualitative or quantitative. Part of its theoretical foundation consists of challenges to the notion of a simple, objective truth.

## 'Discourse research doesn't have practical applications'

Again, this is a common criticism of qualitative research in general. As with some of the other criticisms discussed above, it rests on two incorrect, or at least debatable, assumptions about other kinds of research: that they can produce factual, non-interpretive knowledge about the social world and people's behaviour, and that they can uncover 'rules' which enable prediction and therefore interventions to produce desirable outcomes. The first point concerns interpretation and was discussed earlier. The second concerns models of the social world.

A useful starting point is that all research is partial, involving selection and abstraction. Research findings which have practical applications are generally based on a predictive model. This reduces complexity to establish fairly simple cause–effect relationships, often with significant success (e.g., in many medical treatments). It is appropriate for some, but not all issues. One way to understand this point is to think about different levels. For example, a thousand people in a street could be studied as separate biological organisms, or separate 'feeling' beings with their own personal histories, or, going up a level, as a group functioning *as* a group (e.g., in response to an event which creates panic), or, up another level, as located within an urban or national environment, as part of a population and so on. The difference here is partly a matter of scale, as if a camera were moving outwards and upwards, but also of the aspects of the person which are being considered. How much heat and carbon dioxide do a thousand bodies radiate? How many, going by population-level statistics, are likely to be female, or under 25, or unemployed, or overweight? These kinds of questions have answers which could, potentially, provide a basis for practical applications, for example, about environmental impact or the provision of street furniture or policing or facilities like public toilets.

In contrast, discourse researchers embrace complexity and assume that social phenomena and social worlds are emergent, as discussed in Chapter 2. They are likely to ask different questions. What do these people believe, for example, about staying healthy? How does that behaviour discriminate against (some) others? What different expectations do they place on women or men? They often explore what a predictive model omits. Unlike researchers who set out to develop predictive models which enable practical interventions, discourse researchers are interested in exploring complex aspects of society and social life which in the first instance are more likely to enhance understanding than interventions. The answers to their questions may have applications, but ones which are less straightforward. For example, Bell's research, discussed in Chapter 3, might usefully indicate why some people would resist lifestyle discourses, even if they were informed relevant cause–effect relationships that have been established, perhaps between improved nutrition and lower recurrence of cancer. (Note: this cause–effect relationship is cited as a hypothetical example only, not a reference to research findings.) In general, the practical applications of discourse analytic research often relate to public education and opinion-forming.

## 'Discourse analysis is out of date'

The term 'discourse analysis' is probably no longer as widely used as it was a decade or two ago. This is partly because in some areas of the social sciences, the theoretical focus on Foucault's work, strongly associated with the term 'discourse', has been succeeded by attention to other theorists. However, as the previous chapters of this book have shown, related methodological approaches remain and continue so one reason why discourse analysis may appear less prominent is that it is now often conducted under different labels. Within social psychology, for example, research in the areas of discursive psychology and rhetorical psychology is a development from the sources which originally referred to discourse analysis. Some narrative analysis similarly builds on discourse analysis (e.g., the narrative-discursive approach used by Stephanie Taylor and Karen Littleton, 2006; 2008). Other social researchers incorporate an analysis of discourse into a differently named research approach, such as ethnography or psychosocial research. Discourse analysis, as it has been presented in this book, is an approach to talk and text data which derives from certain premises: language is constitutive, meanings are socially derived and also situated, negotiated and co-constructed and language use is a functional social practice. These notions will continue to underpin the work of many researchers, even if they do not label their work 'discourse analysis'. This book has argued that its value as an analytic approach lies in its breadth and flexibility.

## Summary

Chapter 6 has addressed some common criticisms of discourse analysis.

# 7 Summary

This book has introduced discourse analysis as a social research approach which involves the close interpretation of language data and language practices. It has shown that there is no one way of doing discourse analysis. The common feature of the various forms discussed in the book is that language data, like talk or documents, is not considered simply for the information it conveys through description. Instead, an analysis considers how language works as communication, its situated functions – what is 'done' by talk or written language in a particular context – and the larger systems or formations of meanings which pre-exist, enable and constrain any instance of language use. These aspects can be explored in different ways, deriving to some extent from different theories and academic disciplines. Chapter 1 introduced discourse analysis and Chapter 2 discussed some of the theories and issues associated with it. It also introduced some of the key concerns of discourse analysts and outlined work in social psychology which has contributed to the popularity of discourse analysis as an empirical research approach.

In Chapter 3, four examples of published discourse research were discussed in detail to show alternative possibilities for analysis. The functional nature of language use can be investigated in terms of construction. The researcher might ask: What is the effect of talking about a problem or issue in terms of certain images or cause–effect relationships, such as when ill health is talked about as the consequence of unhealthy living? (This question is addressed in one of the studies discussed in the chapter.) Function can also be explored in an analysis of talk as interaction. A question here might be: How do people complain? How is complaining 'done' in order to sound plausible and appropriate? And how is this accomplished in conversation, between speakers? Or how is leadership enacted? What leadership practices are effective in a common workplace situation like chairing a meeting? Function can also be linked to a certain kind of argument and rhetoric. Possible questions here might be: How does language function to include or exclude certain categories of people? How does such language have effects beyond words? How is racism 'done', for example, in political talk?

Researchers who analyse larger systems of meaning may discuss these in different terms, for example as discourses, Membership Categorization Devices or discursive resources like interpretative repertoires. Some of these terms are associated with distinct named approaches to discourse analysis, such as Critical Discourse Analysis, Conversation Analysis or critical discursive psychology. This book has not attempted to separate these completely. Instead, the aim has been to show the assumptions and foci operating in different studies, regarding these as variants on discourse analysis as it was defined at the start of the book, that is, as 'the close study of language and language use as evidence of aspects of society and social life'. Researchers developing their own projects are likely to follow the example of previous work but also shape their own approaches as appropriate to their topics and investigations.

Why might they use discourse analysis? Chapter 4 set out a number of possible reasons. For many researchers, the attraction and interest of discourse analysis derives from the data. The chapter discussed different types of discourse data and the most common ways to obtain them. It noted that some analysts work with already existing 'found' data while others collect new material. The procedures for data collection are not necessarily different to those entailed in other forms of social research which use language material. Indeed, there is considerable overlap between discourse analysis, ethnography, narrative analysis and other qualitative approaches. (Some of this overlap was discussed in previous chapters.) Because so many researchers are interested in working with interview material, the chapter discussed some potentially distinctive features around interviewing for a discourse analytic project. It also presented an introductory guide to transcription.

Any empirical research presents challenges. Chapter 5 discusses some aspects of discourse analytic research which are likely to concern a novice researcher. In particular, the chapter presented a detailed guide to the process of analysis, from beginning to work with the data to developing an interpretation and argument. This section included accounts of the steps followed on two actual projects, by a researcher working on her doctoral project and two researchers collaborating on a relatively large project employing a research assistant.

Discourse analysis has been a popular form of research for several decades. During that time it has been subject to criticisms, for instance, that it is 'just' about words and that it fails to take account of some other aspects of people and society. There has also been criticism of the most common form of data collection associated with it, interviewing. Chapter 6 addressed these points and others, arguing against the criticisms and showing the continuing relevance of discourse analysis for social research.

# Further reading

New discourse analytic research is likely to be published in the journals *Discourse & Society, Discourse Studies, Critical Discourse Studies, Text, Narrative Inquiry, Qualitative Research, Qualitative Research in Psychology* and, with a more substantive focus, in *Sociological Research Online, The Sociological Review* and many other sociology, social psychology and education journals. The reading list below suggests some relevant books which are likely to be available in a university library. Most are well-established, even classic texts so not particularly new. It also includes some important journal articles.

There are many available texts on discourse research and discourse analysis, some providing the kind of general overview presented in this book and some with a more specific focus.

Two large collections which cover similar ground to that presented (much more briefly) in this book are as follows.
Wetherell, M., Taylor, S. and Yates, S. J. (eds) (2001), *Discourse: Theory and Practice*, London: Sage.
Wetherell, M., Taylor, S. and Yates, S. J. (eds) (2001), *Discourse as Data*, London: Sage.
As the titles indicate, the first collection provides theoretical background with a combination of new writing and reprints from classic theory sources and empirical studies. The second collection presents more general guidance on empirical research and a series of 'workshop' chapters in which researchers present examples of data analysis.

Two highly readable texts which provide a fuller introduction to the social nature of language are as follows.
Fairclough, N. (2001b), *Language and Ideology*, Harlow: Pearson Education.
Hodge, R. and Kress, G. (1988), *Social Semiotics*, Cambridge: Polity.

A series of Sociolinguistic Readers published in 1998 provide an introduction to many of the aspects of discourse analysis and Critical Discourse Analysis which are of interest to sociolinguists and educationalists. They include

Cheshire, J. (ed.) (1998), *The Sociolinguistics Reader Volume 2: Gender and Discourse*, London: Hodder Arnold.

A general guide to Critical Discourse Analysis is provided by the following.

Wodak, R. and Meyer, M. (eds) (2009), *Methods for Critical Discourse Analysis*, London: Sage.

Useful introductions to some of the theorists and theories discussed in Chapter 2 are provided by the following.

Blackman, L., Cromby, J., Hook, D., Papadopoulos, D. and Walkerdine, V. (2008), 'Editorial: Creating subjectivities', *Subjectivity* 22: 1–27.

Burr. V. (2003), *Social Constructionism*, London: Routledge.

Downing, L. (2008), *The Cambridge Introduction to Foucault*, Cambridge: Cambridge University Press.

Lynch, M. (2011), 'Harold Garfinkel obituary: Sociologist who delved into the minutiae of daily life', *The Guardian* 13 July, www.guardian.co.uk/education/2011/jul/13/harold-garfinkel-obituary.

The following text provides a very clear introduction to ethnomethodology and a guide to the uses and advantages of different research approaches.

Have, P. t. (2004), *Understanding Qualitative Research and Ethnomethodology*, London: Sage.

A critical comparison of conversation analysis and (one form of) discourse analysis is presented in the following.

Wooffitt, R. (2005), *Conversation Analysis and Discourse Analysis: A Comparative and Critical Introduction*, London: Sage.

The practical applications of discourse analysis are discussed in the following title.

Willig, C. (1999), *Applied Discourse Analysis: Social and Psychological Interventions*, London: Open University Press.

And also in the concluding chapter of one of the collections mentioned earlier.

Taylor, S. (2001), 'Evaluating and applying discourse analytic research', in M. Wetherell, S. Taylor and S. J. Yates (eds), *Discourse as Data: A Guide for Analysis*, London: Sage and The Open University.

A debate on the use of interviews is presented in the following articles.
Potter, J. and Hepburn, A. (2005), 'Qualitative interviews in psychology: Problems and possibilities', *Qualitative Research in Psychology* 2: 281–307.
Smith, J. A., Hollway, W. and Mishler, E. G. (2005), 'Commentaries on Potter and Hepburn, "Qualitative interviews in psychology: Problems and possibilities"', *Qualitative Research in Psychology* 2: 309–18.

The most famous transcription notation system was developed by Gail Jefferson but this is more detailed than many discourse analytic studies require. Useful discussions on the principles of transcription are contained in the following.
Hammersley, M. (2010), 'Reproducing or constructing? Some questions about transcription in social research', *Qualitative Research* 10(5): 553–69.
Nikander, P. (2008), 'Working with transcripts and translated data', *Qualitative Research in Psychology* 5(3): 225–31.
The second article by Pirjo Nikander particularly addresses issues around discourse analyses of translated data.

The following sources specifically concern discourse research on gender.
Edley, N. and Wetherell, M. (1995), *Men in Perspective: Practice, Power and Identity*, Hemel Hempstead: Prentice Hall/Harvester Wheatsheaf.
Speer, S. A. and Stokoe, E. (2011), *Conversation and Gender*, Cambridge: Cambridge University Press.
Weatherall, A. (2002), *Gender, Language and Discourse*, Hove: Routledge.
Wodak, R. (ed.) (1997), *Gender and Discourse*, London: Sage.

As this book has indicated, many of the best-known texts and studies on discourse analysis have been written by social psychologists. An early and now classic book which introduced discourse analysis into psychology is the following.
Potter, J. and Wetherell, M. (1987), *Discourse and Social Psychology: Beyond Attitudes and Behaviour*, London: Sage.

Other important sources from social and discursive psychology which present slightly different positions are as follows.

Benwell, B. and Stokoe, E. (2006), *Discourse and Identity*, Edinburgh: Edinburgh University Press.

Billig, M. (1996), *Arguing and Thinking: A Rhetorical Approach to Social Psychology* (new ed.), New York: Cambridge.

—(1999b). 'Whose terms? Whose ordinariness? Rhetoric and ideology in Conversation Analysis', *Discourse & Society* 10(4): 543–82.

Billig, M., Condor, S., Edwards, D., Gane, M., Middleton, D. and Radley, A. (1988), *Ideological Dilemmas*, London: Sage.

Edwards, D. (1997), *Discourse and Cognition*, London: Sage.

Edwards, D. and Potter, J. (1992), *Discursive Psychology*, London: Sage.

The following sources develop new approaches for empirical research which are broadly based on the forms of discourse analysis discussed in this book.

(1) Visual research methods

Barker, M., Richards, C. and Bowes-Catton, H. (2012), 'Visualizing experience: Using creative research methods with members of sexual communities', in C. Phellas (ed.), *Researching Non-Heterosexual Sexualities*, Farnham: Ashgate.

Henwood, K., Shirani,F. and Finn, M. (2011), 'So you think we've moved, changed, the representation got more what? Methodological and analytical reflections on visual (photo-elicitation) methods used in the Men as Fathers study', in P. Reavey (ed.), *Visual Methods in Psychology: Using and Interpreting Images in Qualitative Research*, London: Routledge.

(2) Narrative analysis

Taylor, S. and Littleton, K. (2006), 'Biographies in talk: A narrative-discursive research approach', *Qualitative Sociology Review* II(1).

(3) Psychosocial research

Hollway, W. and Jefferson, T. (2000), *Doing Qualitative Research Differently: Free Association, Narrative and the Interview Method*, London: Sage.

# Glossary

**Analysis**

In this book, analysis refers to the close investigation of empirical material (data) as potential evidence for the workings of society. It is therefore a process of exploration with the aim of discovery. The researcher studies the details of data and then considers their wider implications. There are different ways of doing this. Any qualitative analysis, including discourse analysis, tends to be time-consuming. It also generally requires the researcher to develop her own explanation of the relationship between the part (the details of the data) and the whole (the social phenomenon or issue which is being investigated).

**Construction**

This term is linked to the assumption that language is not a neutral vehicle of communication. To talk, or write, about something, or someone, involves choices about words and perspectives and associations. Alternative versions are always possible. For example, a street could be described in terms of its buildings, or trees and gardens, or the people who live there, or of different activities associated with it. Each description constructs the street differently. Discourse analysts are interested in construction as a process, and in the constructed, and co-constructed, nature of people's accounts, and the implications or effects of particular discursive constructions.

**Conversation analysis**

Conversation analysis (CA) is based on the work of the sociologist Harvey Sacks, and its subsequent development by Emanuel Schegloff and Gail Jefferson. It involves the close analysis of talk as interaction, following the principles of ethnomethodology (see Chapter 2). The focus is on details of speakers' utterances and responses within the context of spoken interaction. Ordinary talk is investigated as a skilled, rule-governed, joint activity in which meanings are established and changed through the minutiae of what is said or not said, and how it is said (e.g., the meanings conferred by pauses or by the talk of two speakers overlapping). Conversation analysts generally work with very detailed transcripts. They focus on the talk itself, excluding background information about the speakers and context unless this is directly invoked in what is said. They regard their analyses as 'technical', that is, as following closely from the evidence of the talk itself, which they contrast with more 'interpretive' analyses by other discourse analysts (see Schegloff, 1997; Wetherell, 2001).

## Critical Discourse Analysis
This term refers to an interdisciplinary approach to the analysis of talk and texts which considers the workings of power in society and the role of language in establishing and perpetuating dominance. Some of the best-known writers associated with Critical Discourse Analysis (CDA) are Teun van Dijk, Norman Fairclough and Ruth Wodak. It generally involves analysis on a number of levels, from linguistic features of a text to its location within a larger social context.

## Critical discursive psychology
This term was formulated by Margaret Wetherell (1998) to describe the approach she developed following her initial work on discourse analysis in psychology (with Jonathan Potter, 1987). Critical discursive psychology (CDP) focuses particularly on ways in which discursive work in talk is implicated with social inequalities and the exercise and contest of the workings of power within larger social contexts. A key aspect of the approach is the analysis of discursive resources, such as interpretative repertoires (see definition). Wetherell's own research has included studies of masculinity and, more recently, affect. Other researchers whose work is associated with this approach are Nigel Edley and Sarah Seymour-Smith.

## Discourse
This is the key term of the book yet also one of the most difficult to define. It can refer to communication, specific language practices and a

complex set or system of meanings which is a resource for language use. As Chapter 2 discusses, many writers have developed definitions of discourse which encompass the foci of different analytic approaches.

## Discourse analysis

Discourse analysis is the close study of language and language use as evidence of aspects of society and social life. It can involve the analysis of language data as communication, practice or selective constructions derived from accrued social meanings.

## Discursive psychology

Many of the most influential texts on discourse analysis and related forms of empirical research, such as psychosocial research, have been written by social psychology academics (e.g., Hollway and Jefferson, 2000). Discourse analysis has led to the development of a new area of psychology, discursive psychology, sometimes referred to as a sub-discipline. Academics working in this area have drawn on theories of discourse and discourse practice in order to challenge many traditional psychological theories of the person and also the kind of 'mental' activities (such as remembering) which are studied by some other psychologists, such as cognitive psychologists.

Discursive psychology encompasses different assumptions and methods, and many discursive psychologists would no longer refer to themselves as discourse analysts. There are areas of overlap but also some points of dispute, for example, about the 'right' kinds of data or the relationship between 'technical' and 'interpretive' analyses.

Critical discursive psychologists such as Margaret Wetherell and Nigel Edley are particularly interested in the issues around power which are associated with the work of Michel Foucault. Many other discursive psychologists, including Jonathan Potter, Derek Edwards and Elizabeth Stokoe work more closely in the tradition of ethnomethodology and conversation analysis.

## Discursive resource

One point of investigation for discourse analysts can be the implications and consequences of discourses, that is, the ways in which ideas, representations (in various media), words and ways of speaking have effects in the social world. For example, to call someone a 'good mother' is to invoke a category which is linked to certain words and activities (including what it excludes, that is, all that is associated with *bad* mothering). It is not a neutral categorization but affective, carrying strong emotional associations and potential implications. These meanings are part of the shared knowledge of members of society, largely carried in language, but not exclusively confined to it. By using a term or speaking in a certain way, a particular speaker can draw on all of this shared knowledge; it is a discursive *resource* for a speaker. Part of the purpose of a discourse analytic study can be to investigate discursive resources. Some analysts discuss discourses as resources. Others may focus on a narrower set or clump of words/ideas/ways of speaking, such as a narrative resource or interpretative repertoire.

## Identity

Discourse analysis is often employed in research into identities. At its simplest, identity refers to who someone 'is', with all the range of possibilities that can encompass, from the person's name to a detailed description including a biography, to the multiple roles that person takes in different situations and relationships. Social researchers may study major identity categories such as gender, race, age, nationality and also more specific identities associated with particular contexts or issues (see 'subject position'). Discourse analytic research on identities, especially by social psychologists, has addressed some of the major problems of the social sciences, such as how every person is both an individual actor with a unique identity and sense of who she or he is, and at the same time a component of a larger society, sharing identities with many others and apparently shaped by the social environment to be typical of her or his class, generation, nationality and so on.

## Identity work

Discourse researchers may study identities in talk, such as the subject positions available to a speaker, or how identities are constructed in talk, for example, when a speaker describes herself or others in a certain way. This kind of talk about identity is often referred to as identity work. The concept is linked to the assumption that identities are partly given by contexts (or 'situated') but also actively contested, constructed, claimed and taken up in ongoing everyday talk and other life practices and interactions.

## Ideological dilemma

The notion of an ideological dilemma (or, more simply, a dilemma) in discursive work comes from the work of Michael Billig and others (Billig et al., 1988). They suggested that commonsense logic is often inherently contradictory, so that speakers may find themselves making claims or arguments which they recognize as inconsistent; they then try to repair the inconsistency or otherwise resolve the problem.

## Interpretative repertoire

Another widely discussed discursive resource is an interpretative repertoire. This has been defined as a 'relatively coherent way . . . of talking about objects and events in the world' (Edley, 2001, p. 198) or, in a somewhat broader definition, 'a culturally familiar and habitual link of argument comprised of recognizable themes, commonplaces and tropes' (Wetherell, 1998, p. 400). It is therefore similar to 'a discourse' but is perhaps more specific and particularly associated with the discussion of data. Researchers who discuss interpretative repertoires are often interested in multiple and conflicting resources and their different implications.

## Narrative resource

One example of a discursive resource could be an established narrative sequence such as the sequence of stages which supposedly constitute a 'normal' relationship and life course: courtship, coupling, parenting, etc. This is not descriptive, since many or even most people's lives do not unfold like this. However, it is normative because it shapes expectations, biographical accounts and identities (for a fuller discussion, see Reynolds and Taylor, 2005), influencing how people talk about their own lives and the lives of others and reinforcing certain social values, including the positive valuing of heterosexuality (i.e., it is heteronormative). One form of discourse analysis is a narrative analysis (or narrative-discursive analysis; for example, Taylor and Littleton, 2006) of narrative resources.

## Rhetorical work

This concept comes from the work of Michael Billig (1987; 1999) who suggests that talk is shaped, sometimes quite subtly, by a wider context of media debates, political discussion and social issues. A speaker's rhetorical work is a reference to this context, perhaps in the form of a response to a challenge or criticism which has not been made in the immediate interaction. For example, a comment which begins 'I'm not a racist but . . .' is acknowledging the possibility that what will be said could be heard as racist or prejudiced and that these positions are widely criticized. A comment like this indicates how the speaker is simultaneously situated in multiple overlapping contexts, as a party to the ongoing conversation, a member of the larger society, an audience to current media debates and so on.

## Social constructionism

Within psychology, social constructionism refers to the tradition of theory and empirical research which emphasizes how people's understandings of themselves and their worlds are not based on how things 'are' but on ideas and meanings current within the society. This is consistent with some of the premises of discourse analysis, such as the constitutive nature of language.

## Subject position

The concept of 'a discourse' carries implications for the nature of the (social) world and also the people within it. For example, a discourse of healthy eating creates certain identities, such as a healthy eater, a bad eater and a good parent who provides a healthy diet for the family. Conversely, the identity of 'bad eater' does not exist without a discourse of healthy eating. The identity associated with a discourse like this is called a subject position. It is a 'position' because it is created by the external framework of the discourse. One possible focus of discourse analysis is the shifting subject positions or positionings which are taken up in talk, often quite subtly, for example, in the way someone speaks (e.g., as an authority) or is spoken to, how a speaker describes herself and so on.

## Subjectivity

This term can combine several different ideas. The contrast between the objective and subjective is, roughly, between the outsider and insider point of view, so that, conventionally, objective knowledge is based on neutral, unemotional observation and subjective knowledge as based on experience, enriched by emotion and personal involvement but perhaps liable to bias. (Most contemporary social scientists would challenge this neat division between the subjective and the objective.) A different notion is of the subject as a person controlled or constrained by larger forces, as in references to a 'political subject' who is in the power of a ruler or government. Social theorists have explored the ways in which people are shaped by, or subject to, the wider socio-historic context. With these associations, subjectivity can refer to the sense and experience of 'who I am' which is produced through a person's position, experience and interactions as a member of society. It has a similar reference to identity but emphasizes the location of a person within larger social systems, subject to the workings of power within those systems. The concept is associated with processes by which ideas and value systems come to be part of people's personal beliefs and morality, that is, from an objective to subjective status. This is sometimes contrasted with 'identity' as the objective, outsider view of the same person, for example, as officially categorized by gender, age, occupation and so on.

### Transcription

For the purposes of analysis, discourse researchers generally convert spoken language and other 'lived' interactions into a written form. This can be done by taking notes during the fieldwork or immediately afterwards. Mostly commonly, however, it involves working from an audio- or audiovisual recording to make a detailed record called a 'transcript'. This usually looks rather like the script of a play, listing each speaker and the main words spoken. Other details will be included depending on the researcher's interest and the analytic approach; the same recording can be transcribed in many different ways. Transcription is always time-consuming. It is inevitably selective and is therefore inseparable from the analytic process through which the researcher focuses on and interprets particular features.

### Trouble

The concept of 'trouble' is particularly associated with discourse analytic research on identities. Discourse analysis necessarily involves the investigation of complexity, for example, because of the multiplicity of available discourses and discursive resources and associated subject positions. This complexity gives rise to conflicts and contradictions, for example, between how a speaker positions herself and is positioned by others, or between a positive and negative valuing of the same identity. This kind of trouble prompts discursive repair, for example, through explanations. Trouble in discursive work is interesting for the analyst because it can draw attention to different discursive resources in play and it can also signal the positive and negative values attached to certain identities.

# Bibliography

Abell, J., Condor, S., Lowe, R. D., Gibson, S. and Stevenson, C. (2007), 'Who ate all the pride? Patriotic sentiment and English national football support', *Nations and Nationalism* 13: 97–116.

Bell, K. (2010), 'Cancer survivorship, mor(t)ality and lifestyle discourses on cancer prevention', *Sociology of Health and Illness* 32: 349–64.

Benwell, B. and Stokoe, E. (2006), *Discourse and Identity*, Edinburgh: Edinburgh University Press.

Billig, M. (1987), *Arguing and Thinking: A Rhetorical Approach to Social Psychology*, Cambridge: Cambridge University Press.

—(1995), *Banal Nationalism*, London: Sage.

—(1996), *Arguing and Thinking: A Rhetorical Approach to Social Psychology*, Cambridge: Cambridge University Press.

—(1999), 'Whose terms? Whose ordinariness? Rhetoric and ideology in Conversation Analysis', *Discourse & Society* 10: 543–82.

Billig, M., Condor, S., Edwards, D., Gane, M., Middleton, D. and Radley, A. (1988), *Ideological Dilemmas*, London: Sage.

Bruner, J. (1990), *Acts of Meaning*, Cambridge, MA: Harvard University Press.

Butler, J. (1990), *Gender Trouble*, London: Routledge.

Byford, J. (2006), 'Distinguishing "anti-Judaism" from "antisemitism": Recent championing of Serbian Bishop Nikolaj Velimirović', *Religion, State & Society* 34(1) : 7–31.

Condor, S. (2011), 'Rebranding Britain? Ideological dilemmas in political appeals to British multiculturalism', in M. Barrett, C. Flood and J. Eade (eds), *Nationalism, Ethnicity, Citizenship: Multidisciplinary Perspectives*, Newcastle: Cambridge Scholars.

Davies, B. and Harré, R. (1990), 'Positioning: The discursive production of selves', *Journal for the Theory of Social Behaviour* 20(1): 43–63.

Dixon, J., Reicher, S. and Foster, D. (1997), 'Ideology, geography, racial exclusion: The squatter camp as "blot on the landscape"', Text 17(3): 317–48.

Edley, N. (2001), 'Analysing masculinity: Interpretative repertoires, subject positions and ideological dilemmas', in M. Wetherell, S. Taylor and S. J. Yates (eds), *Discourse as Data: A Guide for Analysis*, London: Sage.

Edley, N. and Wetherell, M. (1995), *Men in Perspective: Practice, Power and Identity*, Hemel Hempstead: Prentice Hall/ Harvester Wheatsheaf.

—(1997), 'Jockeying for position: The construction of masculine identities', *Discourse & Society* 8: 203–17.

Edwards, D. (1997), *Discourse and Cognition*, London: Sage.

—(1998), 'The relevant thing about her: Social identity categories in use' in C. Antaki and S. Widdicombe (eds), *Identities in Talk*, London: Sage.

Edwards, D. and Middleton, D. (1986), 'Joint remembering: Constructing an account of shared experience through conversational discourse', *Discourse Processes* 9: 423–59.

Edwards, D. and Potter, J. (1992), *Discursive Psychology*, London: Sage.

Edwards, D., Ashmore, M. and Potter, J. (1995), 'Death and furniture: The rhetoric, politics, and theology of bottom line arguments against relativism', *History of the Human Sciences* 8(2), 25–49.

Fairclough, N. (2001a), *Language and Power*, 2nd edn, London: Longman.

—(2001b), *Language and Ideology*, Harlow: Pearson Education Limited.

Foucault, M. (2001), *Madness and Civilization*, London: Routledge.

Gee, J. (1992), *The Social Mind: Language, Ideology and Social Practice*, New York: Bergin and Garvey.

Gergen, K. J. (1985), 'The social constructionist movement in modern psychology', *American Psychologist* 40: 266–75.

Gilbert, G. and Mulkay, M. (1984), *Opening Pandora's Box: A Sociological Analysis of Scientists' Discourse*, Cambridge: Cambridge University Press.

Gill, R. (2008), 'Empowerment/sexism: Figuring female sexual agency in contemporary advertising', *Feminism & Psychology* 18: 35–60.

Goodwin, C. (1994), 'Professional vision', *American Anthropologist* 96: 606–33.

Hall, S. (1992), 'The west and the rest', in S. Hall and B. Gieben (eds), *Formations of Modernity*, Cambridge: Polity Press/The Open University.

Hammersley, M. (1998), 'Get real! A defence of realism', in P. Hodkinson (ed.), *The Nature of Educational Research: Realism, Relativism, or Post-Modernism?* Manchester: Manchester Metropolitan University.

—(2010), 'Reproducing or constructing? Some questions about transcription in social research', *Qualitative Research* 10(5): 553–69.

Hammersley, M. and Atkinson, P. (2007), *Ethnography: Principles in Practice*, London and New York: Routledge.

Harré, R. and Gillett, G. (1994), *The Discursive Mind*, Thousand Oaks, California: Sage.

Have, P. t. (2004), *Understanding Qualitative Research and Ethnomethodology*, London: Sage.

Herman, D. (2007), 'Storytelling and the sciences of the mind: Cognitive narratology, discursive psychology, and narratives in face-to-face interaction', *Narrative* 15: 306–34.

Hollway, W. (1998), 'Gender differences and the production of subjectivity' in J. Henriques, W. Hollway, C. Urwin, C. Venn and V. Walkerdine (eds), *Changing the Subject: Psychology, Social Regulation and Subjectivity*, London and New York: Routledge.

Hollway, W. and Jefferson, T. (2000), *Doing Qualitative Research Differently: Free Association, Narrative and the Interview Method*, London: Sage.

Horton-Salway, M., Montague, J., Wiggins, S., and Seymour-Smith, S. (2008), 'Mapping the components of the telephone conference: An analysis of tutorial talk at a distance learning institution', *Discourse Studies* 10(6): 737–58.

Jefferson, G. (1992), (ed.), *Harvey Sacks: Lectures on Conversation*, Cambridge, MA: Blackwell.

Jones, R. L. (2003), 'Older women talking about sex: A discursive analysis', PhD Thesis, Milton Keynes: The Open University.

Kress, G. (2001), 'From Saussure to critical sociolinguistics: The turn towards a social view of language', in M. Wetherell, S. Taylor, and S. Yates (eds), *Discourse Theory and Practice*, London: Sage.

Lawler, S. (2008), *Identity: Sociological Perspectives*, Cambridge: Polity.

McAvoy, J. (2009), 'Negotiating constructions of success and failure: Women in mid-life and formations of subject, subjectivity and identity', PhD thesis, Milton Keynes: The Open University.

Mulkay, M. (1985), *The Word and the World: Explorations in the Form of Sociological Analysis*, London: Allen Unwin.

Nikander, P. (2012), 'Interviews as discourse data', in J. A. Holstein and
    J. Gubrium (eds), *Handbook of Interview Research*, London: Sage.
Ochs, E. (1979), 'Transcription as Theory', in E. Ochs and B. Schieffelin (eds),
    *Developmental Pragmatics*, London: Academic Press.
Onions, C. (ed.) (1965), *The Shorter Oxford English Dictionary*, Oxford:
    Clarendon Press.
Phoenix, A. and Pattynama, P. (2006), 'Intersectionality', *European Journal
    of Women's Studies*, 13: 187–92.
Potter, J. and Hepburn, A. (2005), 'Qualitative interviews in psychology:
    Problems and possibilities', *Qualitative Research in Psychology* 2:
    281–307.
Potter, J. and Wetherell, M. (1987), *Discourse and Social Psychology: Beyond
    Attitudes and Behaviour*, London: Sage.
Raghuram, P. (2009), 'Migration: Changing, connecting and making places',
    in S. Taylor, S. Hinchliffe, J. Clarke and S. Bromley (eds), *Exploring Social
    Lives*, Milton Keynes: The Open University.
Reynolds, J. (2006), 'Patterns in the telling: Single women's intimate
    relationships with men', *Sociological Research Online* 11(3).
—(2008), *The Single Woman: A Discursive Investigation*, Hove: Routledge.
Reynolds, J. and Taylor, S. (2005), 'Narrating singleness: Life stories and
    deficit identities', *Narrative Inquiry* 15: 197–215.
Rose, N. (1989), *Governing the Soul: The Shaping of the Private Self*, London
    and New York: Routledge.
—(1996), *Inventing Our Selves: Psychology, Power and Personhood*,
    Cambridge: Cambridge University Press.
Scharff, C. (2008), 'Doing class: A discursive and ethnomethodological
    approach', special issue: Class and discourse, *Critical Discourse Studies*
    5(4), 331–43.
—(2011), 'Towards a pluralist methodological approach: Combining
    performativity theory, discursive psychology and theories of affect',
    *Qualitative Research in Psychology* 8(2): 210–21.
Schegloff, E. A. (1997), 'Whose text? Whose context?' *Discourse & Society* 8:
    165–87.
Scully, M. (2009), 'Plastic and Proud? Discourses of Authenticity among the
    Second-Generation Irish in England', *Psychology & Society* 2(2): 124–35.
—(2010), 'Local identification and authenticity among the Irish diaspora
    in England', in L. De Pretto, G. Macri and C. Wong (eds), *Diasporas:
    Revisiting & Discovering*, Oxford: Inter-Disciplinary Press.

Seymour-Smith, S. (2008), 'Illness as an occasion for storytelling: Social influences in narrating the masculine self to an unseen audience', in C. Horrocks, K. Milnes, B. Roberts and D. Robinson (eds), *Narrative, Memory and Life Transitions*, Huddersfield: Huddersfield University Press.

Seymour-Smith, S., Wetherell, M. and Phoenix, A. (2002), 'My wife ordered me to come!: A discursive analysis of doctors' and nurses' accounts of men's use of general practitioners', *The Journal of Health Psychology* 7(3): 253–68.

Smith, J. A., Hollway, W. and Mishler, E. G. (2005), 'Commentaries on Potter and Hepburn, "Qualitative Interviews in psychology: Problems and possibilities"', *Qualitative Research in Psychology* 2: 309–18.

Speer, S. A. and Stokoe, E. (2011), *Conversation and Gender*, Cambridge: Cambridge University Press.

Stokoe, E. H. (2003), 'Mothers, Single Women and Sluts: Gender, Morality and Membership Categorization in Neighbour Disputes', *Feminism & Psychology* 13: 317–44.

—(2010), 'I'm not gonna hit a lady: Membership categorization and men's denials of violence towards women', *Discourse & Society* 21: 59–82.

Taylor, S. (2001a), 'Evaluating and applying discourse analytic research', in M. Wetherell, S. Taylor and S. J. Yates (eds), *Discourse as Data: A Guide for Analysis*, London: Sage and The Open University.

—(2001b), 'Locating and conducting discourse analytic research', in M. Wetherell, S. Taylor and S. J. Yates (eds), *Discourse as Data: A Guide for Analysis*, London: Sage and The Open University.

—(2006), 'Attitudes', in D. Landridge and S. Taylor (eds), *Critical Readings in Social Psychology*, London: Open University Press.

—(2007), 'Narrative as construction and discursive resource', in M. Bamberg (ed.), *Narrative – State of the Art*, Amsterdam/Philadelphia: John Benjamins.

—(2010), *Narratives of Identity and Place*, London: Routledge Psychology Press.

—(2011), 'Negotiating oppositions and uncertainties: Gendered conflicts in creative identity work', *Feminism & Psychology* 21(3): 354–71.

—(2012), '"One participant said . . .": The implications of quotations from biographical talk', *Qualitative Research* 12(4): 388–401.

Taylor, S. and Littleton, K. (2006), 'Biographies in talk: A narrative-discursive research approach', *Qualitative Sociology Review* II.

—(2008), *Creative Careers and Non-Traditional Trajectories*, National Arts Learning Network.

—(2012), *Contemporary Identities of Creativity and Creative Work*, Farnham: Ashgate.

Van Den Berg, H., Wetherell, M. and Houtkoop, H. (eds) (2003), *Analyzing Racist Discourse*, Cambridge: Cambridge University Press.

van Dijk, T. (1998), 'Principles of critical discourse analysis', in J. Cheshire and P. Trudgill (eds), *The Sociolinguistics Reader Volume 2: Gender and Discourse*, London: Arnold.

Wertsch, J. (1990), *Voices in the Mind: A Sociocultural Approach to Mediated Action*, London: Harvester Wheatsheaf.

Weatherall, A. (2002), *Gender, Language and Discourse*, Hove: Routledge.

Wetherell, M. (1998), 'Positioning and interpretative repertoires: Conversation analysis and post-structuralism in dialogue', *Discourse & Society* 9: 387–412.

—(2001), 'Debates in discourse research', in M. Wetherell, S. Taylor and S. J. Yates, *Discourse Theory and Practice*, London: Sage.

—(2003), 'Paranoia, ambivalence and discursive practices: Concepts of position and positioning in psychoanalysis and discursive psychology', in R. Harré and F. Moghaddam (eds), *The Self and Others: Positioning Individuals and Groups in Personal, Political and Cultural Contexts*, Westport, CT: Praegar.

—(2012), *Affect and Emotion: A New Social Science Understanding*, London: Sage.

Wetherell, M. and Potter, J. (1992), *Mapping the Language of Racism*, Hemel Hempstead: Harvester Wheatsheaf.

Wiggins, S. (2004), 'Good for 'you': Generic and individual healthy eating advice in family mealtimes', *Journal of Health Psychology* 9: 535–48.

Willig, C. (1999), *Applied Discourse Analysis: Social and Psychological Interventions*, London: Open University Press.

Wodak, R. (2007), 'What is critical discourse analysis? Ruth Wodak in conversation with Gavin Kendall', *Forum: Qualitative Social Research* 8(2): 29.

Wodak, R., Kwon. W. and Clarke, I. (2011), '"Getting people on board": Discursive leadership for consensus building in team meetings', *Discourse & Society* 22(5): 592–644.

Wooffitt, R. (2005), *Conversation Analysis and Discourse Analysis: A Comparative and Critical Introduction*, London: Sage.

Yates, S. (2001), 'Researching internet interaction: Sociolinguistics and corpus analysis', in M. Wetherell, S. Taylor and S. Yates (eds), *Discourse as Data: A Guide for Analysis*, London: Sage.

# Index